# Ben

## Plays: 1

### Gasping, Silly Cow, Popcorn

*Gasping*: 'A sharp-witted satire on the heartlessness of market forces . . . this is the kind of improbable hypothesis that Aristophanes and Ben Jonson relished as the starting point for a play and Elton displays some of their talent for pursuing an idea to its demented logical conclusion.' *Independent*

*Silly Cow*: 'It has an ingenious plot – even as the plot keeps surprising you, however, it also stays funny.' *Financial Times*

*Popcorn*: 'an enjoyable, intelligent, thought-provoking play.' *Independent*
'It thrills on stage precisely because it adopts the sick humour, sickening violence and downright sexiness of the Stone-Tarantino school of film-making that Elton is satirising.' *Evening Standard*
'is far and away the best new comedy in town, as well as the most thoughtful . . . as fresh and crackly as its title . . . as much of a problem play as any ever devised by Wilde or Shaw.' *Spectator*

**Ben Elton** has without doubt established himself as the leading figure in the generation of British comedy stars who emerged in the 1980s. He first achieved prominence when he co-wrote the groundbreaking smash hit BBC situation comedy *The Young Ones*. Ben then went on to write for all the principle comedians of his generation with hit series such as *Happy Families* and *Filthy Rich* and *Catflap*. In 1985 Ben began his phenomenally successful writing partnership with Richard Curtis, writing the award-winning *Blackadder* series and in 1995 he wrote and produced another award-winning comedy series *The Thin Blue Line*. Ben has written best selling novels and in 1996 The Crime Writers' Association awarded *Popcorn* the Gold Dagger Award for Fiction. Ben's stage plays have enjoyed enormous success both in the regions and London's West End and *Popcorn*, having won the TMA Barclay's Theatre Award for Best New Play in 1997, went on to win the prestigious Laurence Olivier Award for Best New Comedy. Ben Elton is best known as a stand-up comedian and his television shows, which he writes himself, have made him a popular and highly regarded comedy performer whose tours are invariably a sell-out, both in the UK and abroad.

# BEN ELTON

# Plays: 1

Gasping

Silly Cow

Popcorn

*introduced by the author*

Methuen Drama

**METHUEN CONTEMPORARY DRAMATISTS**

This collection first published in the United Kingdom in 1998
By Methuen Publishing Limited
Random House, 20 Vauxhall Bridge Road, London SW1V 2SA

1 3 5 7 9 10 8 6 4 2

Random House Australia (Pty) Limited
20 Alfred Street, Milsons Point, Sydney, New South Wales 20561, Australia

Random House New Zealand Limited
18 Poland Road, Glenfield, Auckland 10, New Zealand

Random House South Africa (Pty) Limited
Endulini, 5A Jubilee Road, Parktown 2193, South Africa

*Gasping* first published by Sphere Books Ltd. in 1990
Copyright © 1990 by Ben Elton
*Silly Cow* first published by Warner Books in 1993
Copyright © 1991 by Stand Up Limited
*Popcorn* first published by Samuel French in 1998
Copyright © 1996 by Stand Up Limited
Collection and Introduction copyright © 1998 by Ben Elton

The right of Ben Elton to be identified as the author of this
work has been asserted by him in accordance with the
Copyright, Designs and Patents Act, 1988.

Methuen Publishing Limited Reg. No.3543167

A CIP catalogue record for this book is available from the British Library

ISBN 0 413 73670 9

Typeset by MATS, Southend-on-Sea, Essex
Printed and bound in Great Britain by
Cox & Wyman Ltd, Reading, Berkshire

**Caution**

# Contents

# Ben Elton
# A Chronology

1981    *The Oxford Road Show* (television performance)

1982    Presenter on TV show *South of Watford*
        *The Young Ones* (TV) co-writer, with Rik Mayall
        and Lise Mayer

1985    *Happy Families* (TV) writer
        *Blackadder* (TV) co-writer with Richard Curtis

1986    *Filthy Rich* and *Catflap* (TV) writer

1987    *Blackadder the Third* (TV) co-writer with Richard
        Curtis
        *Motormouth* (album) released on Phonogram

1987–8  *Saturday Night Live* and *Friday Night Live* (TV) host

1988    *Motorvation* (album) released on Phonogram

1989    *Blackadder Goes Forth* (TV) co-writer with
        Richard Curtis
        *Stark*, novel, published by Sphere books.

1990    *The Man From Auntie* (TV) writer and performer
        *Gasping* (theatre), writer, Theatre Royal
        Haymarket, London
        *The Very Best of Ben Elton Live* (video) released on
        Virgin video
        *A Farties Guide to the Man from Auntie* (video)
        released on BBC Enterprises

1991    *Silly Cow* (theatre), writer and director, Theatre
        Royal Haymarket, London
        *Gridlock* (novel) published by Sphere Books
        *Gasping* (play) published by Samuel French

1993    *Stark* (TV) writer and performer
        *This Other Eden* (novel) published by Simon &
        Schuster
        *Silly Cow* (play) published by Samuel French
        *Ben Elton Live 1993* (video) released on Vision
        Video
        *Much Ado About Nothing* (film), actor, directed by

Kenneth Branagh

| 1994 | *The Man from Auntie* (TV) writer/performer |
| 1995 | *The Thin Blue Line* (TV) writer/BBC sitcom with Rowan Atkinson |
| 1996 | *The Thin Blue Line* (TV) writer/second series |
| | *Popcorn* (theatre) writer, Nottingham Playhouse and West Yorkshire Playhouse |
| | *Popcorn* (novel) published by Simon & Schuster |
| 1997 | *Popcorn* (theatre) Apollo Theatre, London |
| | *Ben Elton Live 1997* (video) released on PNE Video |
| | *Ben Elton Live 1997* (album) released on Penguin |
| 1998 | *Blast From the Past* (theatre) writer, presented at West Yorkshire Playhouse |
| | *Blast From the Past* (novel) published by Transworld |

# Introduction

It is a real thrill for me to be able to welcome you to this omnibus edition of my first three plays. Although in fact these are not my first three plays at all, fortunately for you. My actual first play was called *Once More With Feeling* which I wrote when I was fifteen. It was a comedy set in an amateur dramatic society. Soon after that I wrote a lengthy drama about Stalin's purges called *The Bear Hunt* and then an irreverent comedy about the life of Christ called *Miracle Play*. So whatever you may think of the plays in this volume, you can see how fortunate you are that at least they are not my first three plays.

These are my first three professionally produced plays and what I want to say is this, if you are putting any of them on, feel free to cut them and mess about with them as you wish. The texts reproduced here are of the plays as they were originally presented in London but personally I think that *Gasping* and *Silly Cow* are too long and can do with a bit of editing. I saw a production of *Gasping* recently in which they cut the squash scene altogether. They also cut the penultimate scene which takes place in the 'breather tube' but they took some of the dialogue from it to put into the final scene. I thought it worked very well and that the show was a lot pacier.

The first half of *Silly Cow* is all set up so it can drag a little. In a recent production the director took the decision to cut the interval and do it as a long one-act play. I think this is a much better idea but it does necessitate a bit of judicious editing. This is not an easy task with *Silly Cow* because most of what is said in the first half is a set-up for what happens in the second half, nonetheless if you can find a few cuts I suggest that you make them.

For me the main problem with *Popcorn* is that the 'debate' at the end can get a bit wordy. In the French production they got round this in a very creative way. In the play as I wrote it, the television camera is simply placed on stage and everybody plays to it. In Paris however, after a few lines of the debate Wayne grabbed the camera in frustration and shouted directly into it. He then plonked the camera on Bill's shoulder indicated that he should follow the dialogue from then on. From that point the 'debate' was mobile and physical and I thought much more exciting.

Well, just a few thoughts, thank you for reading my plays, I hope that you find them interesting and fun.

Ben Elton
London August 1998

# Gasping

## Characters

**Philip**, *youngish*
**Chief**, *old*
**Sandy**, *young*
**Miss Hodges**, *young*
**Kirsten**, *young*
**Weather Woman**, *young*
**Minister**, *middle-aged*
**Reporter**, *youngish*

And the taped voices of **Voice Over, Announcer's Voice, DJ, Little Jenny's Voice, Mum's Voice**

The action of the play takes place in a variety of locations

**Time**: 1990*

*'Dated' references could be changed if required

**Gasping** was first presented by Phil McIntyre by arrangement with Proscenium Productions at the Theatre Royal Haymarket, London, on 1st June 1990, with the following cast:

| | |
|---|---|
| **Philip** | Hugh Laurie |
| **Sir Chiffley Lockheart (Chief)** | Bernard Hill |
| **Sandy** | Simon Mattacks |
| **Miss Hodges** | Catherine McQueen |
| **Kirsten** | Jaye Griffiths |
| **Weather Woman/ Minister/Reporter** | Catherine McQueen |

With the voice of Stephen Fry

*Directed by* Bob Spiers
*Designed by* Terry Parsons
*Lighting by* Mark Henderson
*Produced by* Philip McIntyre

# Act One

## Scene one

*The executive boardroom of Lockheart Holdings.*
*A power office with large panoramic windows. A strategy meeting*
*is in progress, with graphs and chart.*
**Philip** and **Sandy**, *two top young execs, are pitching to Sir*
*Chiffley Lockheart, the* **Chief**.

**Philip**  And so, Chief, as you can see, all divisions are
way way ahead of seasonal predictions. Look, (*He takes a
graph.*) this is my biggest graph and Peter Profit is way
way off the right hand corner . . . I've had to glue two
together . . . (*He proudly folds it out.*) Well, obviously I
didn't do it. I had some of my people do it. Anyway,
whoever did it, the results, as I think you'll agree, are
impressive. Our corporate hem-line is showing off
plenty of stunning thigh. If this keeps up much longer
we're going to have to move into a very much bigger
pair of corporate trousers. Possibly Switzerland.

**Chief** (*slightly confused by* **Philip**'s *language*)  Hmm, yes,
can I just get this clear, Philip. We're making money? Is
that what you're trying to say?

**Philip**  Senior money, Chief. If *God* wanted to buy
into Lockheart stock, he'd have to think twice *and* talk to
his people.

**Chief**  Good. Good, at least I think good. So, taking a
broad view, Philip, charts and presentation rubbish
aside, what's your personal gut reaction?

**Philip** (*thoughtfully pacing*)  Well, Chief, I would have to
say, that I am very excited. In fact I have said it, I said it

to my people only this morning, 'People,' I said, 'I am very excited,' and they know I don't mince about the bush. But it isn't just me, Chief, the sales task force is very excited. The boys in corporate raiding are very excited. The market strike unit damage control spin doctors are very excited. Above all, Chief, *you* should be excited . . . Sir Chiffley Lockheart should feel like a twelve-year-old who's just discovered it's not only for pissing.

*A phone rings.* **Philip** *and* **Sandy** *instantly produce portable phones.*

**Philip**⎱
**Sandy**⎰ (*together*)   Not now, goddammit.

*The phone rings again.* **Chief** *calmly picks up one of the phones on his desk.*

**Chief** (*into the phone*)   Thank you, Miss Hodges, could you possibly hold all calls? Thank you . . . (*He hangs up and crosses to the champagne trolley, fingering bottles.*) And you, Sandy, how do you feel about our corporate erection? Are you as excited as Philip?

**Sandy**   Well, Chief, I wouldn't want to commit myself fully until I'd talked to my people, but off the cuff, as a non-binding, ball park reaction, I'd say that if anything I was slightly more excited than Philip.

**Chief**   More excited?

**Sandy**   Slightly, Sir.

**Chief**   I see. (*He pauses.*) Unfortunately, I'm not.

**Sandy**   Slightly more excited than Philip in one way, Sir . . . but in twelve other ways, rather less so . . . (*He stifles a yawn.*)

**Philip** (*after a surprised pause*)   Chief, I'm just not in following mode here. I mean, look at the graph! We couldn't be making any more money if we were a lesbian couple with six test-tube kids living off the social security in a Labour controlled borough while the Home Office tried to send us back to Sri Lanka.

**Chief** Please don't misunderstand me, Philip. I'm pleased, good Lord yes, oh no question there. It's just that I'm not excited.

**Philip** You're not?

**Chief** I couldn't be less excited if you were both Swedish.

**Philip** (*pulling himself together*) Chief, you're absolutely right. OK, so Peter Profit has opened up his dirty mac and said, 'What about that for a whopper'. But hell, there are bigger girls in the cat-house down the street and they can squat down and pick up ping-pong balls! And what's more, without using their hands. We have to meet Terry Triumph and Derek Disaster and treat those two impostors just the same.

**Sandy** Chief's right, Phil. Champagne? Forget it, mine's a cup of coffee, very black and I'm on to my next video ledger heading for the right hand column with my decimal point in my hand.

**Philip** (*packing up his visual aids*) Sorry to have wasted your time, Chief. We'll be back when this red line (*He points at the graph.*) is wound round the room so often you'd think it was a Blue Peter Christmas appeal . . .

*They are about to go.*

**Chief** (*stopping them*) Don't be absurd, our profits are quite magnificent. I'm delighted with them. But you have to face facts. There is nothing remotely exciting about our present success. We make our huge piles of money by *having* huge piles of money. We buy land, take over factories, invest in other people's labour and creative zeal.

**Philip** and **Sandy** are rather crushed.

(*Reflecting for a moment; he has something significant to tell them.*) Gentlemen, I'm no longer a young man, but my life so far has been a full one. I've seen a great deal and I've bought almost all of it. I've hobbed with the rich and I've nobbed with the beautiful. Do you want to know what is exciting? (*After a pause.*) The Pot Noodle. That's what's exciting. Find me a Pot Noodle, *then* you shall see your old Chief excited.

*There is a brief pause for surprise.*

**Philip** (*pacing across the room, hitting the intercom*)   Daphne, get your sweet little ass in here pronto dammit, with some Norris Noodles, instant variety, assorted flavours and why the *hell* wasn't this anticipated. You're paid to *think* goddammit . . . (*He turns the intercom off.*) All sorted, Chief, I can't imagine how it got overlooked.

**Chief** moves to the intercom.

**Chief** (*into the intercom*)   Cancel the last request, Miss Hodges. I should explain, Philip, that I am employing a metaphor . . .

**Philip**   You won't find I have a problem with that, Chief: if a guy's good, I don't care where his parents were born.

**Chief** (*with an arm round* **Philip**)   Philip come over here, let me show you something.

**Philip**   With you, Chief.

**Chief**   It's a painting by Rembrandt, who as you may be aware, was a painter. It is a torso.

*They cross to the wall where a picture hangs.*

**Philip** (*wishing to convey awe-struck delight*)    Oh . . . Oh
Sir, oh oh oh, *Chief* . . . it's exquisite, Sir, quite
exquisite . . . the, uhm, colour and the . . . light, yes,
that's it, the light. Am I right, Sandy? Back me up.

**Sandy**    No question, Philip, the guy had senior talent.
The sort of rough-hewn, fierce-eyed, canvas-covering
cowboy who'd get up in the morning and say to his
shaving mirror, 'I *can* paint. I *will* paint'. By mid-
afternoon he's holding a major retrospective and he's
*bored*.

**Philip**    Exactly! Chief, let me tell you a little about the
way I see this guy. Come five thirty on the West bank of
the Seine, when all the other smock-wearers are packing
up their brushes ready for another evening of booze,
whores, and trying to come to terms with being only
three feet tall, friend Rembrandt power-packs another
paletteful, phones the Louvre, tells them to clear a wall
and before you know it, the *Mona Lisa*'s winking that
inscrutable wink at him while her ears dry.

**Chief**    You're an admirer, then?

**Philip**    Be a fool not to be, Chief. The fact that
Rembrandt had access to real business-class ability is *not*
negotiable. Christ, you only have to look at the guy's
product. (*He indicates the canvas.*)

**Chief**    Well, you may be right, I'm sure you are, but
as it happens, this isn't the picture. This is the picture of
the bright purple Spanish girl in the nude that some
clever so-and-so sells millions of every year. The
Rembrandt's behind it. (*He pushes a button.*)

*The picture rises up, to reveal a second picture set in the wall.*

What do you think?

**Philip**   . . . And this one's the Rembrandt, is it?

**Chief**   It is.

**Philip**   Oh, oh Chief, oh oh oh, *Chief* . . . it's exquisite, Sir, quite exquisite . . .

**Chief**   The light and the colour good?

**Philip**   Terrific.

**Chief**   Good, because this pretty little Dutch girl cost me seventy-two million pounds.

**Philip** *and* **Sandy** *gasp.*

I think they saw me coming, what do you think?

**Philip**   We-ell, I suppose it is a substantial *wad* to lay out for a piccy, but you're a 'can do, must have' kind of guy, Sir. Sandy?

**Sandy**   When Sir Chiffley Lockheart says 'I want', the price tag does *not* have a seat at the negotiating table.

**Chief**   The point I am trying to make, gentlemen, is that this (*He indicates the painting.*) is a Pot Noodle. And this . . . (*He takes the Spanish picture.*) by a matter of coincidence is also a Pot Noodle. Do you want to know what a Pot Noodle is?

**Philip**   Uhm . . . it's a painting?

**Chief**   A Pot Noodle is the most beautiful thing on Earth. It is a new way of making money. A way of making money . . . *where no money existed before*: the very definition of excitement.

**Philip**   Look, I'm probably being thicker than a middle manager's filofax here, Chief, but I'm just not in an 'understanding you' mode at all. Uhm . . . what *is* a Pot Noodle?

**Chief**   It's a large plastic cup containing chemically-saturated dried spaghetti and peas to which the consumer is instructed to add boiling water.

**Philip**   Ye-e-s . . . and perhaps you could talk me through the significance factor on this one . . .

**Chief**   The most unlikely food stuff in history. When they launched it nobody gave it a chance . . . Nonetheless, against all expectations the market not only absorbed it, but embraced it. There was no drop in sales of any other form of food. Money had been generated where *no money existed before*.

**Philip** (*very impressed*)   And all because of one bonkers, iron-willed troubleshooter who put his balls into a cup of spaghetti.

**Chief**   Only the British could market Pot Noodle, because only the British would eat them. That unknown marketing hero had faith in the concrete, rat-like digestive system of the British consumer and he's been in profit since day one.

**Philip**   My God, Chief, that's probably the most inspirational anecdote I've come across since I first leafed through my Gideon in a *Holiday Inn*.

**Chief**   Pot Noodles come in all shapes and sizes. This picture is worth seventy-two million because that's what I paid for it, nothing to do with its intrinsic value. There's probably more light and colour in a packet of fruit flavoured Polos. What makes the thing so special is that when I sell it, the bidding will *start* at seventy-two million. This (*He indicates the Spanish painting.*) is a Pot Noodle . . . Who could possibly have predicted that anyone would want anything so ugly, and yet some brilliant fellow thought of printing them on to hardboard and getting Woolworth's to stock them next to the Pick'n'Mix. Anyone worth their company BMW can carve a bigger share of an existing market, but show me the person who can make a pound where there was *no pound to be made*. That's the fellow who's going to be sitting alongside me and the Board in the executive jacuzzi whirlpool bath.

**Philip**   The executive Jason, Chief, that's a mightily big carrot!

**Chief**   Find me a Pot Noodle and you're in it, Philip, what's more, you can sit on one of the jets. Find me a Pot Noodle!! Bring the excitement back! Make me some money where no money existed. Make an old man happy!!

*Black-out.*


**Scene Two**

*The sounds of a squash court, the huge grunting of the players, the banging of the ball, followed by anguished shouts of self loathing: Hur! – Bonk Hur! – Bonk hur! – Bonk . . . Hell, bugger it!!' Hur! – Bonk Hur! – Bonk hur! – Bonk . . . 'Oh, for* Christ's *sake what the* hell *am I* doing!' *Hur! – Bonk Hur! – Bonk hur! – Bonk . . . 'Come* on, *God, I'm playing like a total prat.' Hur! – Bonk Hur! – Bonk hur! – Bonk . . . 'Bollocks!'*

*The lights come up on* **Sandy** *and* **Philip**, *down stage in squash gear. They put their phones down. They have rackets but they mime the ball They face outwards towards the audience who are the back wall.*

**Philip**   Well, I must say I'm looking forward to a couple of punishing points of 'wallop the bollock', eh, Sandy?

**Sandy** In likewise mode, Philip!

*They warm up, etc.*

**Philip** Feeling pretty trim, actually – by bugger I've pumped so much iron lately you could melt me down and beat me into a canteen of cutlery.

**Sandy** I'll lob one up, shall I?

**Philip** Give it your best shot, young Sandy.

**Sandy** (*miming a hard serve with a grunt*) Huuurrrr!!

*We hear two bonk sounds as **Sandy** hits the imaginary ball, then the ball hits the wall.*

**Philip** (*miming a return with an even bigger grunt*) Huuurrr!!!

**Philip** *bobs about as if ready to return again, but* **Sandy** *has relaxed and is looking behind him at the ground. It is clear that despite* **Philip***'s huge lunge and grunt, he missed his shot completely.*

**Sandy** Out.

**Philip** (*realizing*) Hmmm, yes, I suppose technically it is, yes, not bad, Sandy, not bad at all, but you're putting far too much curve on it. Try to imagine that there's an invisible string attaching your right wrist to your left ear. Here, look, I'll show you. (*He picks up the imaginary ball and plays a shot with a huge grunt.*)

*Bonk.*

**Sandy** *returns, bonk,* **Philip** *lunges, grunts and misses again.*

You forgot the string, Sandy, you're not concentrating, are you? You'd better serve, give you the edge.

**Sandy** Right you are, love-all then.

**Philip** Love-all it is.

**Sandy** *is about to serve,* **Philip** *stops him.*

Of course, I can't blame you for being off your stroke after the session we had with the Chief this morning. He certainly is an inspiration.

**Sandy**   Mmm. So it's love-all.

**Philip**   And not likely to change until you serve, old scout.

**Sandy** *(giving him a look and then serving)*   Hurrr!

*Bonk.*

**Philip**   I mean, working the . . .

*The ball hits the wall – bonk.*

. . . kind of hours I do . . . *(He returns.)*

*Bonk.*

. . . fellow needs a passion . . .

. . . *The ball hits the wall – bonk.*

. . . for some people there's always birds I suppose . . .

**Sandy** *returns – bonk.*

. . . but not me. I've no time for totty.

*The ball hits the wall – bonk.*

Ha!!! *(He makes a huge lunge and swipe, and misses.)*

*The ball goes dibbly dibbly.*

**Sandy**   One-love.

**Philip**   Mmmm, did you see what I was trying to show you there? Cross-court wrong foot, well worth picking up.

**Sandy** *(picking up the ball and preparing the serve)*   One-love.

**Philip**   Technically, yes.

**Sandy** (*serving*)   Hurrrr!

*Bonk.*

**Philip**   Quite frankly . . .

*The ball hits the wall – bonk.*

. . . if I do make totty time . . . (*He hits the ball.*)

*Bonk.*

. . . the ruddy girl's . . .

*The ball hits the wall – bonk.*

. . . always busy. Amazing . . .

*It was lob,* **Sandy** *watches it land, turns round and plays it off the back wall – bonk.*

(*Turning round as well.*) Ah, now your problem is . . .

*The ball hits the wall – bonk. They both turn out again; the ball goes dibbly, dibbly.*

**Sandy**   My point.

**Philip**   Ye-es, but it could so easily not have been . . . I played my drop plonker shot into your gutter.

**Sandy**   Two-love. (*He walks forward to pick up the ball.*)

**Philip**   So there you were with my plonker in your gutter and you go to pieces, start looking the wrong way and God knows what. Can't blame you really it is pretty disconcerting when one considers just how ruddy busy girls are these days. Sometimes I can't believe how busy they are.

**Sandy**   I find they can usually make time. Two-love. (*He serves.*) Hurr!

*Bonk.*

**Philip**    Actually we're lucky really . . .

*The ball hits the wall – bonk.*

. . . more time to . . . (*He hits the ball.*)

*Bonk.*

. . . forge that career . . .

*The ball hits the wall – bonk.*

. . . dream those dreams.

**Sandy** *hits the ball – bonk.*

Sir Chiffley gave us . . .

*The ball hits the wall – bonk.*

. . . a dream today . . .

**Sandy** *hits the ball very hard – bonk. Almost immediately it hits the wall – bonk.* **Philip** *lunges, misses, we hear it hit the side wall – bonk,* **Philip** *lunges feebly as the ball hits three other walls – bonk, bonk bonk. Finally it goes dibbly dibbly.*

You see, Sandy, that was all over the place.

**Sandy**    Three-love.

**Philip**    I don't blame you for being distracted. What an inspiration the old man is. Just imagine it, Sandy, aeroplanes were Pot Noodles once, and artificial limbs. Hang on to that, it'll see you through when the bulls turn into bears and some secretary's put herbal tea in the Kenco. By crikey, it'd be a pretty strange fellow who could get lonely doing the sort of big, important job we do. Quite frankly I don't have *time* to get lonely.

**Sandy**    It's three-love. Are you ready . . .

**Philip**    No, bugger it! We've got work to do! (*He slaps* **Sandy** *on the back and walks off.*) Come on, soldier, bugger your introspection, if you want to be a philosopher, get a job with Channel Four. We've got arses to kick. So we'll call it a draw, eh?

**Scene Three**

*Sir Chiffley's office, as in Scene One*

*It is a month later; a plant or two may have flowered.*

*The* **Chief** *and* **Miss Hodges**.

**Chief** (*perhaps just the slightest hint of adjusting tie*)    Thank you, Miss Hodges, that was beautifully done. I don't think I've ever known a secretary who could handle a ledger quite like you can.

**Miss Hodges**    It's kind of you to say so, Sir Chiffley.

**Chief**    And such a very heavy one.

**Miss Hodges**    I'm glad of the exercise, Sir.

**Chief**    Do you think it's worth going through it again?

**Miss Hodges**    Well, Sir, you had scheduled a brainstorming session . . .

**Chief** (*glancing at his watch*)    What? Good Lord yes, that excited memo from young Philip . . . Is he here?

**Miss Hodges**    He's outside, Sir.

**Chief**    Well, send him in, girl, send him in.

**Miss Hodges**    Certainly, Sir Chiffley.

**Miss Hodges** *exits.*

*Sir Chiffley pats the ledger.*

**Philip** *enters, carrying a mobile phone.*

**Philip** (*into the phone*)    Hold all calls.

**Chief**    Sorry to keep you waiting, Philip, but I've been considering your memo and I must say it confused me slightly. You say here, (*He refers to the memo.*) you've grabbed the challenge by the balls and sunk your teeth into it. Does this mean you have an idea?

**Philip**    Chief, my metaphorical balls are so lacerated you'd think I had a hypothetical crocodile in my trousers. As you know, it's been a few months since you outlined the Pot Noodle brief and I don't mind admitting that those few months have been about as fertile as a dead eunuch.

**Chief**    But no longer.

**Philip**    I think not, Sir. You're probably aware that we recently acquired the Associated London Press . . .

**Chief** (*thoughtfully*)    Publishing . . . Publishing . . . Yes, good, I'm interested. Not desperately original of course, been done before, but so has bending over a roll-top desk and getting your secretary to beat you on the bottom with a really heavy ledger, and I certainly don't let that stop me.

**Philip**    And why should you.

**Chief**    Associated London is a perfectly decent group of newspapers. All we have to do is turn them into vicious, semi-pornographic, right wing toilet paper and we'll make a mint. Of course, Rupert Murdoch will sue us for conceptual plagiarism but it's all good publicity . . .

**Philip**    Uhm, actually Chief, I'm targeting something a little more specific here . . .

**Chief**   I see, well let's have it then, lad.

**Philip**   Well Sir, I was checking out the titles we'd acquired, looking for a decent male, adult-interest magazine . . . They have some bloody interesting articles about vintage sports cars in those male, adult-interest magazines, you know.

**Chief**   Of course they do, and there's nothing dirty or shameful in that.

**Philip**   I suppose I was trying to get my mind off noodles . . . but no go, I'm afraid. (*He paces.*) I was restless, fretful, I could feel it, I could smell it . . .

**Chief** (*slightly doubtful*)   Now then, Philip, I'm confused, are we still talking about your idea here. Or have we moved on to male, adult-interest magazines?

**Philip**   Still the idea Chief . . . I knew it was close . . . I'd seen something in one of the papers, but I couldn't recall . . . The little Vodaphone I keep in the back of my head was trying to dial me, but I guess my brain must have been in a meeting . . . Then suddenly . . .

**Chief**   Your brain took the call!

**Philip**   Exactly! The paper I'd been trying to remember was a magazine for hay fever sufferers. (*He produces the magazine.*) *The People's Hay Fever Listener Examiner Gazette Magazine – Phlegm.* (*He hands it over.*) Or to put it another way; a Pot Noodle. It says here, Chief, and get this . . . they have just invented a machine which is guaranteed to suck in pollen-infested air, extract the pollen, and blow the air out again!!

**Chief** (*after a pause*)   Well frankly, Philip, I'm a little disappointed. This is very junior stuff. Of course, we can purchase the patent on this machine if you wish, put the price through the roof. I have no objection to milking a few snot noses.

**Philip**　Hmm, yes, but . . .

**Chief** (*enthusiastically*)　If I am under any moral obligation to offer a bunch of streamy-eyed sneeze merchants an easy ride, then I am unaware of it.

**Philip**　I was . . .

**Chief**　No dew-drop-hanging free-loader chewing on a mouthful of mucus need expect the feather-bed treatment from Lockheart Holdings.

**Philip**　I should say not, but . . .

**Chief**　Yes, certainly, go ahead, nail those phlegm-heads to the wall and empty their pockets. If they want pollen-free air, make 'em pay. But really, Philip, your secretary should be doing this sort of thing for you.

**Philip**　Chief, hear me out! It says here that the machine takes the oxygen from the air, cleans it, and stores it ready for when Cyril Snotnose feels a tickle coming on, when he can give himself a blast of pure, cool oxygen . . .

**Chief**　Stores oxygen? What, like a scuba tank?

**Philip** (*very excited*)　Yes, but more so . . . the ad says it incorporates a revolutionary compression process which allows considerable quantities of oxygen to be extracted from the air, and stored for when the sufferer needs to flood the environment with pure nose-fodder.

**Chief** (*still doubtful*)　We-ell, interesting concept, I suppose . . . could sell well to marine research, it might even perhaps have some applications in space, but I really don't see . . .

**Philip** (*very excited*)　Chief, think bigger, think

stunningly big, think first-class cabin baggage allowance. What I am talking about here is *designer air*!

**Chief** (*after a huge pause*)    My God, it's enormous.

**Philip**    I've done some research in sister fields, Sir. Water for instance, you can have no concept how big the ponce water market is, and after all, when you come down to it, what *is* Perrier? A multi-million pound industry, selling people stuff that falls out of the sky. The French must be absolutely pissing themselves, that's probably what gives the stuff its acrid taste.

**Chief** (*beginning to get excited too*)    My dear boy, I think you may have stumbled on something absolutely colossal here, talk me through your thinking so far.

**Philip**    Picture our target consumer, right? I had graphics knock me together some visual backup. (*He has visual aids, computer graphics, etc. He pieces together or somehow produces a full-size cut-out of a yuppie with a briefcase.*) His career is in ascendant mode, his other car really *is* a Porsche. He wants the very best and he intends to get it.

**Chief**    I like him already.

**Philip**    He has a home gym that looks like an iron-lung factory. His yogurt is so alive it shuts the fridge door for him. His muesli is coarse enough to prize open the buttocks of a concrete elephant and his chickens are so free-range he meets them for drinks at his club. And what is he breathing? What is he breathing, Chief?

**Chief**    You tell me, Philip, you've done the research.

**Philip**    Bus drivers' farts! That's what he's breathing. He is breathing the same stuff that people in the North are burping their Vimto into. Have you any idea of the cocktail of natural fumes a dog emits when it's on heat . . . ?

**Chief**   Pretty gruesome I should imagine.

**Philip**   There are guys out there pulling down six figure incomes being forced to breathe that stuff! Something has to be done.

**Chief** (*hitting the intercom*)   Hold all calls, please, Miss Hodges, and alert security if you'd be so kind, we have a potential Pot Noodle in the building . . . Carry on, Philip.

**Philip**   Picture it, Chief. You have two wine bars, OK? Both are so crowded it takes three days to get a drink. Both have got girls slooshing the plonk with legs sufficiently frisky to revitalize the British motor industry. Both have got a large blackboard that says something indecipherable about game pie . . . But get this, only *one* is offering pure, sparkling, guaranteed filtered, cleansed and mineral-enriched *private* air. Now which hostelry do you think our free-wheeling troubleshooter who wants the *best* is going to patronize?

**Chief**   Philip, this one, if I might be forgiven some exuberance, is a stallion's stiffy.

**Philip**   It's a whale's whopper.

**Chief**   It's an elephant's appendage.

**Philip**   It's a dinosaur's dong.

**Chief**   It's the giant's giblets. How do we go about acquiring the thing?

**Philip**   Chief, I'm way, way ahead of you. You're still training for nineteen ninety-two in Barcelona, I'm on my way to Manchester for ninety-six. I have bought up the patent in perpetuity. I also took the liberty of indoctrinating one or two junior top-level executives into the project. (*He hits the intercom.*) Sandy, bring in Suck and Blow.

**Chief**    I like it.

**Sandy** *enters with the machine.*

**Philip**    I suggest that for this demonstration we implement a complete security shut down . . . windows, doors, intercom . . . this thing could be bigger than food.

**Chief**    And food is very big. Activate the shut down, Philip.

**Philip**    Sandy, get your butt on it, for Chrissakes.

**Sandy** (*not really enjoying being addressed in this manner*) You got it, Philip. (*He hits a button.*)

*Huge steel screens descend in front of each window and door.*

**Philip** (*bustling round the machine, turning on lights and moving bits*)    Now then, the chemical reaction which extracts the oxygen is similar in many ways to photosynthesis; it creates gaseous carbon compounds which compensate for the loss of the oxygen in the atmos, so there shouldn't be a pressure drop. But watch out all the same.

**Sandy**    Pressure doesn't worry me, Philip, I am a walking area of high pressure. When I go outside, the weather changes.

**Chief**    I like this young fellow, Philip.

**Philip**    My top man, Sir, believe me, he's being groomed.

**Sandy**    If people get too close to me their ears start bleeding.

**Philip**    Yes, all right, Sandy, let's hit Barry Button. (*He presses a button.*)

*The machine begins to whirr and hum and flash, steam comes out of it, and a small balloon begins to inflate.*

The oxygen is now being extracted, Chief, in a few minutes it will all be inside the machine.

**Sandy**    Uhm, Philip . . .

**Philip**    Later, Sandy.

**Sandy**    No, really, Philip . . .

**Philip**    Not now, Sandy.

**Sandy**    It's just that, if the machine is extracting all the oxygen from the atmosphere, what are we going to breathe?

**Chief**    Good point, young fellow.

**Philip**    I encourage all our people to come up with good points, Chief.

**Chief**    Good. Are you grooming him?

**Philip**    Like he was a horse, Sir.

**Sandy**    I'm not sure it's working actually, nothing very much seems to be happening. (*His knees buckle.*)

**Philip**    Get up, Sandy, stop playing the giddy ass. (*He collapses.*) Sorry Sir, ruck in the carpet.

**Chief** (*gripping the desk unsteadily*)    What the devil is going on!

**Sandy** (*pulling himself up unsteadily*)    I think it's the machine, Sir, we don't notice we're suffocating because the replacement elements fool the lungs into believing that they are breathing normally.

**Philip** (*crawling to his feet*)    Sandy, are you trying to say that we have stupid lungs; because, if so I take a pretty dim view . . .

**Chief**    I'm getting dizzy, somebody open a window or I shall sack the lot of you!

*All are very wobbly and faint.*

**Philip** (*trying to pull up a metal screen*)    They're all on the security timer, Sir . . .

**Sandy**    I'll call Miss Hodges . . . (*He moves to the intercom.*) hallo . . . hallo . . . She can't hear me, the damn thing's on security shut-off too . . . !

**Philip**    Techno let-down. Try upping the volume on your natural communication system.

**Sandy**    What?

**Philip**    Shout.

**Sandy** (*squeaking*)    Help . . . help . . . I'm not sure I can, Philip . . .

**Chief** (*struggling to get the words out*)    If anyone can think of something sensible they will be making a most advantageous career move . . .

*The machine is now grunting and shaking. The balloon is full.*

**Sandy**    Well, it's just a thought, but we pressed the button marked 'suck'; maybe we should press the one marked 'blow' . . .

**Philip** (*lying prostrate on his back, staring upwards; faintly*)    I was wondering how long it would take you to notice that, Sandy. Well done, memo me to intensify your grooming process . . .

**Sandy** *staggers to the button, presses it, and the whirring changes. The balloon quickly deflates. Almost instantly they all go 'Aaaaaah' with relief.*

Obviously the instruction manual will have to be very clear on certain points.

*Black-out.*

**Scene Four**

*The office of Image Control, a top advertising agency.*
*Total cool, designer work place, with big glossy blow-up photos*
*taken from previous campaigns.*

**Kirsten Carlton**, *a top ad lady.*

**Kirsten** (*into the phone*)   No, dammit, Anton, I can't see
you! This is a major pitch for me, Lockheart are
launching an entirely new product and I want the
bloody account . . . Listen, if you can't handle sleeping
with someone in a higher income bracket I'll bike you
round a bloody bimbo! Don't bother to call! (*She slams
the phone down and hits the intercom.*) Graham darling, send
in the gentlemen from Lockheart.

**Philip** *and* **Sandy** *enter.*

**Philip**   Kirsten, at long last, I'm Philip, this is my top
man Sandy . . . I can call you Kirsten? You give such
good fax I feel I almost know you, anyway formalities
are totally inefficient. Whoever said 'manners cost
nothing' never had to play hard ball across eight time
zones with the Tokyo stock exchange.

**Sandy**   Those guys are tough.

**Philip**   *Terry* Tough! By the time you've said
'greetings honourable colleagues', they've bought your
company, miniaturized your lawn mower and eaten
your goldfish.

**Kirsten**   Phil, Sand, let me tell you something about
me. People tend to address me in one of two ways – it's
either 'Kirsten', or 'that tough bitch', you can have it
whichever, whichways, whatever way you want it.

**Philip** (*laughing*)   I think we're going to get along just
fine, Kirsty.

**Kirsten**  When you come to Image Control, you come to the best. The media is a minefield of no-talent, sad-act companies whose address is a portable fax machine on the back seat of a Mini Metro.

**Philip**  Exactly.

**Kirsten**  You do *not* require some member-munching mincer with a Design Centre security laminate on his tit . . .

**Philip** *grunts with exasperated recognition.*

. . . a Marks and Spencer *crudité*s dip in the saddle bag of his ten-speed racer . . .

*Again* **Philip** *understands.*

. . . and an ad concept featuring a basking iguana, an enigmatic male model and no mention whatsoever of the actual product because that would be naff.

**Philip**  God, you've met them too?

**Kirsten**  You've come to us because we empty shelves.

**Philip**  That's what the word is on the streets. I play squash with a guy from Imperial Biscuits who says you brought the Jammy Dodger back from the dead.

**Kirsten**  I had a small, chemically produced biscuit with a blob of red sticky stuff in the middle of it and my cute little ass was on the *line*. Imperial had given me a *donger* of a budget to push the Jammy Dodger up-market, get it out of the tuck shop and into the executive dining room.

**Philip**  It was inspired, I'll never forget it, Penelope Keith pushing the wafer mints away . . . (*With a plummy voice.*) 'Pass a Dodger, Roger'.

**Sandy**   Brilliant casting, Nigel Havers as Roger was just so stylish.

**Kirsten**   Disappointing in bed, surprisingly.

**Philip**   Hmm, yes, well anyway . . . Sandy, I believe you've accessed Kirsty on the relevant base-line information and she's Suck and Blow compatible.

**Kirsten** (*gathering her visual aids together*)   Sandy's good, Phil, very good.

**Philip**   Believe me, he's being groomed. Now then, Kirsty, I'm not going to pussyfoot around here, I respect you too much and know you have no time for feet in your pussy so tell me, how do you feel about Suck and Blow?

**Kirsten**   Suck and Blow is the most exciting product I've encountered since the Pot Noodle.

**Philip**   Did you hear that, Sandy? Rendezvous with destiny or what! This lady worked on the Pot Noodle!

**Kirsten**   My first job . . . 'Put on the kettle, Gretel.'

**Sandy**   'Fill my pot, Dot.'

**Kirsten** (*touched*)   You remember it.

**Philip**   I feel *very* good about this project, let's have lunch!

**Sandy**   Uhm, perhaps we should ask Kirsten if she's had any time to come up with some ideas yet?

**Philip**   Oh come on, Sandy! You've only just accessed here.

**Kirsten**   I like to work fast, Phil, I toyed for a while with 'Share my air, Claire', but I think it's time to go radical . . . Let me run this byline past you . . . 'Other people's air, it'll get right up your nose'.

*Short pause; they are thrilled.*

**Sandy**   It's . . . brilliant! Quite brilliant!

**Philip**   There's a rare and savage beauty to your copy, Kirsty.

**Kirsten** (*briskly assembling story boards, presentation portfolios, etc.*)   I'd want to use the fellow who does the Creamy Churn Dairy Spread voice-overs, he turned round their whole campaign with that quiet, sinister way he has . . . (*She hits a button.*)

*We hear a tape: 'Half the calories of butter or margarine, but all the buttery taste . . .'*

**Philip** (*excited*)   I buy the damn stuff myself! . . . (*Correcting himself.*) I mean, it always seems to be in the fridge . . . I've got this absolute treasure, I'd probably look totally *Biafran* without her.

**Kirsten** (*handing over a designer folder*)   You'll find the text on blue . . . We saturate local radio for a fortnight, classic rock and current affairs stations only, of course – not a lot of point pitching to some twelve-year-old heavy metal fan whose testicles are still somewhere in the region of his armpits.

**Philip**   With you on that. What about the telly?

**Kirsten**   I've been thinking hard about television . . . Let's try a little word association game, Philip, just for the fun of it, throw me back your instant reactions, OK . . . Class.

**Philip** (*instant list*)   Bogart, Chivas Regal, Sergeant Pepper, Harley Davidson, Johann Amadeus Bach, mist on a moonlit lake, friendship.

**Kirsten**   You missed something out, Philip.

**Philip**   I did?

**Kirsten**   Sandy?

**Sandy**   Suck and Blow?

**Kirsten**   Exactly.

**Philip** (*short pause, slightly miffed*)   Hmm, yes well, I rather thought that went without saying.

**Kirsten**   Nothing goes without saying in advertising, Philip, think of Coca Cola. We all *know* it adds life and is the real thing, we don't need reminding that it unites the world, and you can't beat the feeling . . .

**Sandy**   It really is an incredibly now beverage.

**Kirsten**   Exactly, but if their agency had made the mistake of imagining those things went without saying, we'd be still under the illusion that Coke was just a sweet, sticky drink that can completely dissolve a tooth inside twenty-two hours.

**Philip**   I hope you're listening to all this, Sandy. Because you're interjecting on a grade 'A' marketing seminar.

**Kirsten**   OK, let's move on to the actual TV time slots. I'm thinking of a sophisticated restaurant scenario here, we're talking real . . .

**Philip**   Class?

**Kirsten**   Exactly.

**Philip**   Wine glasses the size of buckets . . .

*Plenty of movement, they act it out.*

**Kirsten**   Only three items on the menu . . .

**Philip**   Portions so small you think you've got a dirty plate and it turns out to be your *main course* . . . (*He gets excited.*) A hundred and fifty pounds for a splash of raspberry sauce with a squiggly vanilla line through the middle . . . We are talking the very *best* in executive dining.

**Kirsten**    Fine, so you have the venue . . . close-up on two young executive lovers having pre-sex dinner. (*She makes a lens of her fingers, as directors are wont to do.*) They are a class act. She is one heck of a lady, essentially romantic, but romantic on *her* terms. She has a body that says 'screw me', but watch out because in business hours she'll screw *you*, and screw you to the *wall*. We're looking at a sort of young Meryl Streep with shades of Sigourney Weaver, Jodie Foster, Cher and Sylvester Stallone.

**Philip**    I like this lady. What about the guy?

**Kirsten**    Let's just say that our high-class chick is thinking about giving up everything to have his children.

**Philip**    I hope he realizes the kind of levels he's lucked out at.

**Kirsten**    He does, he's one heck of a guy . . . Sandy, you read 'man in restaurant'; I'll read 'sexy girl' . . . (*She gives him a designer folder.*)

**Philip**    Uhm, hang on, uhm . . . don't you think it would be better if I read 'man in restaurant'? Just a thought.

**Kirsten**    OK, you get the part, try it very Michael Douglas. (*She sits at a convenient table, and acts.*) 'So darling, next stop the Tokyo posting.'

**Philip**    Right, OK, here goes . . . (*He acts.*) 'I'm afraid not darling, they've given Tokyo to Simon.'

**Kirsten** (*acting*)    'But you're by far the best man . . .'

**Philip** (*acting*)    'I'm afraid you're going to miss out on all the perks. The magnificent access to Far Eastern shopping facilities, the gorgeous little Sushi bars, the Samurai servants . . .'

**Kirsten** (*acting*)   'Such a shame you didn't get it.'

**Philip** (*acting*)   'Oh, I got it all right, I just didn't take it. The office doesn't have Suck and Blow.'

**Kirsten**   And then the voice-over comes in, imagine the man from the Dairy Spread commercials . . . (*She hits the tape recording.*)

*The tape: 'Remember, a man prepared to breathe second-rate air will probably be prepared to deliver second-rate product. If your people deserve it, fit Suck and Blow.'*

**Philip** (*thrilled*)   But this is wonderful, I mean absolutely Barry Brilliant! Just totally and utterly Barry!

**Kirsten**   It has class, Philip.

**Philip**   It has more class than a *Sunday Times* Wine Club special selection case.

**Kirsten** (*handing out more groovy designer folders*)   Item Two uses a similar couple, in a power seduction situation. It's his flat and the lady is hot, right? The coffee and Armagnac are all through and she's just about ready to climb aboard and rut her horny little ass off. She just wants to bang her gorgeous, muscly, workaholic, over-achieving boyfriend till his dick falls off.

**Philip**   Ha ha, believe me, I've been that guy.

**Kirsten**   Then you'd better read it again. (*She slaps another groovy designer folder across at him.*)

**Philip**   Sorry, Sandy, perks of seniority . . .

**Kirsten**   (*acting*) 'Mmm, lovely coffee . . . I must say

you seem to have everything in your beautiful
apartment . . . the best food . . . the best wine . . . Only
the best of everything, I like that in a man.'

**Philip** (*acting*)    'There's a pool on the roof, I thought
we might swim a little later . . .' (*Aside to* **Sandy**.) This is
*superb*!

**Kirsten** (*acting*)    'As long as it's secluded . . . I don't
have a swimsuit. (*She sniffs.*) Is something burning? . . .
Apart from me that is.'

**Philip** (*aside to* **Sandy**)    I can't believe this stuff, it's
just *so* believable . . . (*He acts.*) 'Ha ha, that's the caviar
and truffle soufflé ruined.'

**Kirsten** (*acting*)    'Never mind, I'm not hungry – for
food, and the Suck and Blow will soon clear the air.'

**Philip** (*acting embarrassed*)    'Uhm . . . hmm . . . yes . . .
I'll just open a window, shall I?'

**Kirsten** (*acting suddenly cold*)    'Is that the time? I really
must be going.' (*She hits the tape recorder.*)

*The tape: 'If you haven't got a Suck and Blow, you haven't got
anything at all.'*

**Philip** (*very excited*)    Kirsten, I don't know what to say.
It's quite simply utterly stunning, it could not be more
quite simply utterly stunning if you'd written it on a
sledge-hammer and bashed young Sandy here over the
head with it. Class, you said? This campaign has more
class than the *Royal Family*!

**Kirsten**    If you can sell the product into the shops
I anticipate commencing a saturation sweep within
a matter of weeks. We should be picking up our
first major advertising industry awards soon after
that.

**Sandy**    It's a magnificent campaign, we'll sweep the board.

**Philip**    A campaign's no use at all without product outreach. Come along, Sandy my son, we've production targets to reach. Check you later, Kirsty.

**Kirsten**    You can always get me on the portable.

**Philip** *and* **Sandy** *exit.*

**Kirsten** *begins to assemble her stuff.*

**Philip** *enters.*

**Philip** (*sincere tone*)    Kirsten, I am a busy man, I did not arrive at where I am today by beating myself with a bush, so I'll put it bluntly. I'm a plain and simple man with plain and simple tastes and I like to see a woman who is both. Can we do dinner?

**Kirsten**    Why not, that would be lovely.

**Philip**    That's OK, no hassle, forget it, I respect a woman who is busy . . . What!

*Black-out. During the darkness we hear a Capital Radio ad break with a fake Suck and Blow ad in the middle.*

**DJ**    And we'll be back with the Capital weather, news of the Help-a-London Child appeal and of course lots more music, after this . . .

*Two or three real ads, followed by . . .*

**Mum's Voice**    Well Jenny, that's the floor done, I've cleaned the house from top to bottom, everything's sparkling and clean for your birthday party.

**Little Jenny's Voice**    No, it isn't, Mummy.

**Mum's Voice** (*laughing indulgently*)    All right, Jenny, what have I missed?

**Jenny**   All the lead, the carbon, the nicotine, the dried dead skin cells, the human methane, oh lots and lots of horrid poisonous muck!

**Mum**   Well, I can't see any of that, dear.

**Jenny**   You can't see it, Mummy, but it's there and I'm going to have the dirtiest, most unhealthy birthday party in my class.

**Voice Over**   Doesn't your child deserve the benefits of Suck and Blow . . . ? Other people's air: it'll get right up your nose.


**Scene Five**

*A steamy massage room.*

*There are a couple of benches for massage.*

*Downstage,* **Philip** *and* **Chief** *wander on with towels wrapped round waists, dripping, wet and sudsy.*

**Chief** (*puffing on a huge cigar*)   So, young fellow, your first dip in the top nobs' jacuzzi whirlpool bath. I'm sure your telephone will be fine when it's dried out a bit.

**Philip**   It's a legal problem now, Chief. When I purchase hardware purporting to be executive level equipment I simply presume that it's whirlpool bath compatible. Surely that has to be the bottom line.

**Chief** (*taking a robe from an imaginary servant*)   Thank you, that will be all . . . (*To* **Philip**.) Absolutely first-class steam-room attendant. Totally respectful. It's not often you get respected as well as that these days, is it, Philip? Respect like that is a rare and precious thing.

**Philip**   Oh, no question, the guy gave really terrific respect. Respect-wise, he's a senior talent, a genuine first-division respecter.

**Chief**   One of the little perks of being at the top, Philip, is being respected as well as that. Respected by people who really know how to respect. You're going to find yourself on the receiving end of that quality of respect more and more often, Philip.

**Philip**   Sounds like pretty heady wine, Chief.

**Chief**   Well, I think you know that you've earned it. You've masterminded a Pot Noodle of quite simply colossal proportions. Suck and Blow is the marketing phenomenon of the decade.

**Philip**   Yes, and even more satisfying than the money, Chief, is that we've improved the quality of people's lives.

**Chief**   Yes, well, of course you're right, the social contribution we're making is nice too . . . (*He addresses an invisible masseur.*) Just oil me up and calm me down, would you, thank you so much . . . (*To another imaginary attendant.*) It's my young friend here's first time so loosen him up a bit, eh? Untie the old muscular knots and bash him into shape, splendid . . . (*He gets on a bench.*) You'll enjoy this, Philip, nothing like a massage to relax you after an executive steam.

**Philip**   Yes, I once had a massage in Bangkok, terrific. (*He gets on the other bench. Discreetly to the imaginary servant.*) Just the straight stuff, OK? Don't bother with the gentleman's executive relief or the lollipop game . . . Mmm, oh yes, most relaxing. (*Trying to imply total relaxation and enjoyment.*) Oh, oh oh oh, *yes*, mmm, that's terrific, mm mmm . . . (*He screams.*) Ahh! (*He flings his legs apart, as if the imaginary masseur was pulling him violently.*)

**Chief** (*comfortably immobile with the cigar*)     Don't worry, he's just breaking down the tissue tension to help you relax.

**Philip**     Fantastic . . . Ahhh!! (*He arches his back violently, speaks with difficulty.*) He's a really terrific relaxer . . . Huhhh!! (*He slams his back down and raises his legs straight in the air, all his weight on his shoulders.*) Uhhh!!

**Chief** (*still puffing on the cigar*)     To the victor the spoils, Philip, if anyone deserves a moment's relaxation, you do.

**Philip** (*straining*)     Major compliment received and appreciated, Chief. Ahhh!! (*He flings his legs all the way over so that his toes are on the bench behind his head, he is completely doubled up.*)

**Chief**     People are choosing to purchase Suck and Blow ahead of CD players, microwaves. We penetrate lower income brackets daily. That's what I admire about you, Philip, you're flexible.

**Philip** (*straining*)     I like to think so, Chief . . . Aaaahh!! (*He does a full backward roll, coming up on his knees. He immediately slams himself face down on the bench.*)

**Chief**     You bend with the marketing wind . . .

**Philip**     I certainly hope so, Chief... Huurrrr!! (*Face down, he lifts his chest and knees from the bench in a banana shape, balanced on his pelvis, then slams down.*) Huurrr!!

**Philip** *does this a number of times while the* **Chief** *carries on.*

**Chief**     You turn with the trends, you're malleable, Philip.

**Philip** (*throwing himself into a headstand*)     Chief, I'm just a cog, just a part of the company machine, but I love the company, and when it comes to shifting company product, I swear I'm ready to slap my balls right on the line, again and again and again.

**Chief**   I'm sure Abdullah would be quite happy to do that for you . . .

**Philip** (*panicked*)   No!! . . . I'd hate to trouble him.

**Chief**   Then perhaps another steam?

**Philip** (*very relieved*)   I'd love one, Chief.

**Chief**   All right, Abdullah, that will do . . .

**Philip** collapses as if he has been held up by the feet and has just been dropped. **Chief** gets up.

Yes, I'm delighted, Philip. Why, even here in the gym, even through the steam it's clear as crystal, one hundred per cent sterilized, pure, private air.

**Philip**   With a hint of damp pine on a dewy morning, if I'm not mistaken.

**Chief**   Let me tell you, Philip, I don't miss the reek of stale truss at all. It's a pleasure to draw breath. As indeed it is in any decent establishment in London these days. (*He walks across and through the steam we see a Suck and Blow machine lurking in the corner. He slaps it appreciatively.*) I salute you. And of course your splendid team. I've been delighted with the advertising campaign, that young girl is a marvel. Terribly firm, I like that. It's frisky.

**Philip**   Kirsten is quite literally the best, Chief. That little lady with the cute little ass could get the Pope to sanction condom machines in confession boxes.

**Chief** (*wryly*)   Am I to presume, Philip, that your fancy is taken?

**Philip**   It's difficult not to be attracted to total excellence, Chief.

**Chief**   I don't normally condone liaisons with contracted employees, Philip. It blurs future negotiations. If you are thinking of getting involved, I beg you to ask yourself the question, could you marry her and sack her on the same day?

**Philip**   I think partners who can't sack each other don't have much of a relationship, do you, Chief?

**Chief**   Well, all right then. But steady, laddie. Clever women take some handling. A beautiful tradesman's entrance takes the eye, then a keen mind picks the pocket.

**Philip**   Well, Chief, I have to say that I see it differently. There's no room in my life for some clueless popsy with a cordon bleu cookery diploma, norkas like melons and a brain like a grape. If that makes me a feminist then I make no apologies, but I'm sorry.

**Chief**   I suppose a lot of you young fellows are feminines these days. Personally, I'm still a bit of an old sexy myself and I don't mind admitting it.

**Philip**   Different generations, Chief, different lifestyle requirements. If I want an attractive cocktail shaker I'll win the corporate squash tournament and get awarded one with my name engraved on it.

**Chief**   It's an attitude I can only admire, Philip. (*Jolly, a bit laddish.*) Well as the saying goes, faint heart never got serviced in a variety of interesting positions and locations so I suggest you stop lolling about, pull on your shreddies and get courting.

**Philip**   Reading you, Chief. (*He gets up.*)

*The steam has cleared.* **Philip** *begins to dress. Perhaps there is a small chest-high screen, or a little block of lockers to do it behind, or else he just does it under a towel.*

**Chief**   So what's your first move, eh? Get her
alone in the conservatory and slip her a box of choccies
with an antique French dildo nestling in the second
layer?

**Philip**   If only.

**Chief**   Too subtle, you think?

**Philip**   Oh no, it's not that, it's just that . . . well, to
tell you the truth, I'm not awfully good when it comes to
talking to totty. Oh, I'm all right with business, but
when it comes to anything remotely gropey, I'm a clam.
I took Kirsten to dinner only last week, and we talked
about nothing but sucking and blowing all evening . . .
Ended up discussing the staff, she nearly managed to
poach Sandy off me, clever bitch . . . I just could not
bring myself to nudge the situation on to more intimate
lines.

**Chief**   Like so many great men before you, a daunting
figure of power and confidence in battle, but a gawking,
shuffling boy in matters fruity, eh?

**Philip**   That's me, Chief. It's a hell of a handicap
when you're trying to unload your cherry, I can tell you,
Sir. I got so tongue-tied on any subject but work that she
actually mentioned it. Said I was hopeless at small talk,
said any girl interested in me would probably have to
pitch in and damn well ask me herself.

**Chief**   Well, whatever the situation is *vis-à-vis* cherry
disposal, Philip, you mustn't let it distract you from the
main task, and that is the continued success of Suck and
Blow. (*He slaps the machine.*) We must be very careful,
we're in danger of becoming victims of that very success.
The Japanese are already in. It hasn't taken those clever
fellows long to strip down a sucker and wrest from it its
secret.

**Philip** (*bitterly*)   And as far as Mr Suzuki-Mitsubushi-the-war-was-nothing-to-do-with-me-squire is concerned, we can stuff our patents-pending right up our polite English bum holes. These people just don't play fair, Chief. Look at what they did to the British motor industry! Deliberately and maliciously destroying it by making better cars. They have a four and a half *million* letter alphabet and they still can't spell the word 'decency'.

**Chief**   Well, you started this, Philip, it is your job to keep us ahead. I'm giving you *full* responsibility, I want you to live, sleep and *breathe* 'air'.

**Philip**   It will be the deepest of privileges, Chief. After all, Suck and Blow isn't just about money. Hell, let the Japs have a piece. We are building the future here, making a better, healthier, cleaner world for our children . . .

**Chief**   Children, eh? I must say this clever little lady with the attractive cul-de-sac certainly seems to have made an impression.

**Philip**   Well, I don't know, Chief, call me a total drip if you like, but things just seem to be so bloody *right* at the moment; major career upswing, beautiful girl . . . As long as I can sort out the old nerves and slip her an offer, that is.

**Chief**   You will, lad, you will, you can't help being sensitive. Now, have you got my briefs?

**Philip**   No question, Chief: live, sleep and *breathe* air. I'm with you.

**Chief**   No, I meant have you got my briefs? These aren't mine, (*He holds up a pair of pants.*) they've got a cartoon representation of a maggot emerging from an apple on the front, and the words 'girl bait'.

**Philip**   What! Good Lord, sorry, Chief, wasn't thinking, sorry. (*He is dressed, checks in his trousers.*) Silly Christmas present, keep meaning to chuck them . . .

**Chief**   Philip, believe me, you're the top coming man, but I don't think you're quite ready to move into my underpants yet, eh?

**Philip**   God forbid, Chief.

**Chief**   I don't need His help, I give my own orders. You've got yours, now give me my skidders, bung on your own, get out there and turn the whole nation into suckers.


**Scene Six**

**Kirsten**'s *office*
*New story boards and stuff. There is a large shiny Suck and Blow in a corner.*

**Philip**   I don't believe this, Kirsten, why it's not two months since the Chief told me to live, sleep and breathe air! There can't be a problem!

**Kirsten**   Philip, I don't care what Sir Chiffley said, I'm telling you, the first surge is over. With the Japs and the Yanks in, competition is getting more intense and demand is falling. We have definitely got a glitch in the gusset.

**Philip**   Hell, bugger.

**Kirsten**   I've got figures to pitch at you that will be harder to swallow than an Aeroflot breakfast.

**Philip**   (*into his portable phone*)   Hold all calls.

**Kirsten**   Sales-wise, my research teams are predicting downswing.

**Philip**    Downswing or Plummet swing?

**Kirsten**    The household and domestic market is dead set to dump faster than an Italian-made kite.

**Philip**    Are you saying that there is a problem with the boom product of the decade?

**Kirsten**    Problem is not a word I like Phil, me and the word 'problem' do not get along. If the word 'problem' were to take me out for the evening I'd be home by nine thirty and curled up with a good book five minutes later.

**Philip**    Well, quite.

**Kirsten**    Nonetheless, production is definitely too high for the current market to absorb. Lockheart have shifted three million units in the UK alone, never mind Sony, Westinghouse, K-Tel. Even the Sinclair model is selling and that pumps nitrogen . . . look at this . . . (*She brings out an enormously thick newspaper of seven or eight inches.*)

**Philip**    A copy of last week's *Sunday Times*. Superb article on arms smuggling, terrific graphic of a huge arrow with a gun drawn on it, going from Iraq to a Semtex factory in Czechoslovakia, made it all so clear . . .

**Kirsten** (*taking a thin section from the huge paper*)    Take a look at Section twenty-seven, part four, the 'Lifestyle' pull-out is devoted entirely to the second-hand Suck and Blowers. The domestic market is saturated, we need to target much more specifically; there are a thousand areas in which people could be persuaded to expect private air. Doctors' waiting rooms, bus stations, theatres, factories.

**Philip**    So you think with the right marketing you can de-glitch the gusset?

**Kirsten**   With the right marketing you can do anything you want, Philip. If we handle this glitch properly, before we know it, Lockheart will make you President of the whole air division . . . but it needs the right marketing. (*With a tiny hint of sauciness.*) And of course with the right marketing . . . girl.

**Philip** (*suddenly nervous*)   . . .Well, we've . . . uhm, I mean *I've* or rather we've, I've, certainly got that, Kirsten. I don't know what Suck and Blow would have done without you.

**Kirsten**   Or me without it. You know, Philip, this campaign has been pretty exciting for me . . . in more ways than one.

**Philip** (*tongue-tied*)   So. (*His voice breaks into squeak.*) How's . . . I'm sorry, (*With a deep voice.*) how's that, Kirsten?

**Kirsten** (*a bit sexily*)   We-ell, let's just put it this way . . . That there's a certain horny chick from Creative Marketing (*She touches him teasingly.*) who's been working pretty closely with a certain hot guy from Lockheart . . . And this certain horny chick reckons this certain *hot* guy is sort of special, OK? You know, a real *tasty geezer*! Are you with me, Phil? (*More flirty touching.*)

**Philip**   Ah, hmm, yes, uhm . . .

**Kirsten**   What's more, I've got a kind of girly suspicion that with the right persuasion he'd rut like a charging elephant and could find a G-spot blindfold with his hands tied behind his back.

**Philip** (*very embarrassed*)   Coo, Harry Hot in here, isn't it? I'll just open a window, shall I?

**Kirsten**   Now don't change the subject . . . anyway, better not, the air's been sucked a bit thin out there today . . . (*She crosses to him.*) But what I want to know, Philip, is do you think I'm right about this hot hunky guy . . . ? After all . . . (*She touches him again.*) you know him much better than I do.

**Philip**    Well I . . . hmmm, yes, elephant, you say? God, I don't know . . . perhaps . . . (*He hurriedly packs his briefcase.*) Look, hell, Kirsten, I've really got to charge, I mean rut, I mean run! Meetings to orgasm, I mean organize. People to sex, see . . . ! Anyway, right, bye!

**Kirsten**    You won't forget what I've said, will you, Philip?

**Philip**    Twelve types of no way, I mean, no way for sure!

*Black-out. In the darkness we hear* **Philip** *cry out in frustration.*

Oh, Barry Bollocks!!!

*We hear the voice of a theatre announcer.*

**Announcer's Voice**    Ladies and gentlemen, before we continue with tonight's performance you may like to know that before our next production, which will be Andrew Lloyd Webber's new musical *Aspects of Mussolini*, this theatre will be fitted with Suck and Blow machinery throughout, so that all our patrons may enjoy the safety and the quality of one hundred per cent filtered private air. Thank you for your attention.


**Scene Seven**

**Sandy** *is walking across the stage, with a briefcase and a portable phone, doing business in the street.*

**Sandy**    Hallo, Gary? Yeah, we won the case, Philip is going to sodding ejaculate! . . . Yeah, the judge ruled parents have the right to switch their kids' schools on air cleanliness grounds, the implications are enormous . . . I really think it's time we started pressing the Home Office on prisons, I mean quite apart from the humanitarian arguments, with minor adjustments it could be a superb way of inputting tear gas . . .

*A ringing sound.*

Oh, bugger, hang on, Gary . . . (*He produces a second phone.*) Yo, Tony! Just talking to Gary . . . (*Into the first phone.*) Gary, it's Tony . . . (*Back to the second phone.*) Tony, can you hold . . . (*Back to the first phone.*) Yo Gary, I'm back . . .

*Another ringing.*

Bugger! Hang on, Gary . . . (*Into the second phone.*) Hang on, Tony . . . (*He produces a third phone.*) Speaking . . . Great, Jurgen, guten tag . . . (*Into the first phone.*) Gaz, it's Jurgen . . . (*Into the second phone.*) Tone, it's Jurgen. (*Into the third phone.*) Listen, Jurgen, I'm just speaking to Gary and Tony . . .

*Another ringing.*

Bollocks . . . (*Into the first phone.*) Hang on, Gaz . . . (*Into the second phone.*) Hang on, Tone . . . (*Into the third phone.*) Eine minute, Jurgo . . . (*He answers the fourth phone.*) . . . Geoff, thanks for getting back . . . (*Into the first phone.*) Gaz it's Geoff . . . (*Into the second phone.*) Tone, it's Geoff . . . (*Into the third phone.*) Jurgo, it's Geoff . . . (*Into the fourth phone.*) Listen, Geoff, you'll have to hold, I'm just talking to Gaz, Tony and Jurgen . . .

*Another ringing.*

Heigh ho. (*Into the first phone.*) Gaz, I'm pulling in a lot of favours here but I'm going to need two ticks' worth of breathing space . . . (*Into the second phone.*) Tone, it's got to

be a peco-sec minimum . . . (*Into the third phone.*) Achtung
Jurgo, look it's a totally Donner und Blitzen situation
over here, I feel like an utter Schweinhund, but you'll
have to hold . . . (*Into the fourth phone.*) Geoff, I've got LA
in one ear, Frankfurt in another, and the Space Shuttle
in a third, be right back . . . (*He produces a fifth phone either
from under a hat or straight out of the Khyber Pass.*) Phil! Yeah,
we won! The anti-air lobby got a serious case of
brewer's droop . . . Phil, give me an eighth of a tick . . .
(*Into the first phone.*) Listen Gaz, talk to Tone. (*He holds both
phones together in one hand. Into the third phone.*) Jurgo?
Sprechen sie mit Geoff, will you? (*He holds the two phones
together in the other hand. The fifth phone is now between his
knees.*) Phil? (*With the briefcase under an arm he begins to bunny-
hop off whilst talking into the fifth phone*). Yeah, you have to
believe it, Phil, their dicks were pointing *south* . . .

*A sixth ringing as the lights fade. This time the ringing is very loud
to cover him hopping off.*

## Scene Eight

*The lights come straight up on the boardroom.*

*There is champagne as in the first scene. The phone continues to
ring from the end of the previous scene.*

**Chief**, **Philip**, *and* **Sandy**. **Sandy** *is demonstrating.*

**Chief** (*interrupting* **Sandy**, *he picks up the phone*)    Not
now, Miss Hodges.

**Sandy**    So as you can see, Chief, I'm very excited;
what I'm barely suppressing here is blue chip, gilt-edged
excitement . . . since Philip and Kirsty bashed out their
deep penetration policy . . .

**Philip** (*distracted*)    If only . . .

**Sandy**   Sorry?

**Philip**   Nothing.

**Sandy**   In the incredibly short time since then, private air has become the bottom line for just about any enclosed space in the country. Sales are soaring steeper than an up-bound Seven-Four-Seven scraper-hopping out of Hong Kong.

**Chief**   Yes, and I think perhaps a small celebration is in order . . . (*He crosses to the drinks trolley.*) Gentlemen, allow me to propose a toast . . . a toast to Philip, the first President of the entire Lockheart Air Division.

**Sandy** (*surprised*)   Hells bells! Senior career upswing! Well done, Philip!

**Philip** (*surprised but a little preoccupied*)   President . . . ! Chief, I had no idea . . . I don't know what to say.

**Chief**   You seem a trifle underwhelmed, my boy.

**Philip**   Oh no way, Chief, I mean absolutely thirty-seven types of no way, Chief!

**Chief**   Philip, I am Sir Chiffley Lockheart. I have more money than God and I am not a fool, please don't treat me as one. What's on your mind?

**Philip** (*slightly taken aback*)   Well I . . .

**Chief**   Come on, out with it, nobody loves a shillier, no more do they a shallier, let us have your thoughts.

**Philip** (*after a moment's hesitation*)   Chief, nobody wants to poop on the parade but I pride myself on being a realist, I like to think I give better realism than an omnibus edition of *EastEnders*. Well, this is where I get real. Chief, the party's over.

**Sandy** (*shocked*)   What!

**Chief**    You surprise me, Philip.

**Philip**    What can I tell you? I am hoovering up stale crisps and trying to get red wine stains out of the shag pile. The party is definitely on its last legs. I don't like it, my people don't like it, but there you are. The problem is, Sir, that the machines store too much. People are strange fish, the capacity exists so they fill it . . . they are stockpiling oxygen. (*He hands out reports.*)

**Chief**    I'm aware of that development, Philip, kindly explain the problem. It's not as if the world is short of oxygen, we'd need literally billions of machines to noticeably affect the make-up of the atmosphere.

**Philip**    Oh, absolutely, Sir, in broad terms there is clearly no problem . . . locally, however, the story can be somewhat different. As you are aware, Sir, when the machines suck in oxygen they create an equal and opposite amount of carbon compounds, hence there is no pressure drop.

**Sandy**    Which has been considered essentially right from the very beginning: no unseasonal winds are created, the weather remains unaffected.

**Philip**    Hmm, yes, unfortunately, until a natural wind blows . . . within the localized environment, where mass sucking is taking place, there can develop a bit of a shortfall on breathing material . . . not for very long, but well, 'not very long' is actually quite a while in respiratory terms . . . It's suddenly all got rather serious, in some areas brief periods have arisen where strolling for a bus has been a similar experience to climbing Mount Everest.

**Sandy** (*looking at the report*)    Unfortunately, without the accompanying exhilaration, sense of personal achievement and potential to capitalize on your name through commercial sponsorship.

**Chief**   I see.

**Philip**   We are beginning to be looking at a potential scenario where grannies could start keeling over in the streets.

**Sandy**   Chief, I have to tell you, that sort of development could be a public relations nightmare.

**Philip**   The same thing's happening abroad. There's a lot of wild talk about massively prohibitive licence fees, possibly even a blanket ban. I very much fear that Suck and Blow is spiralling into Dodo mode.

**Chief**   I see. You're clearly rather depressed about this, Philip. What about you, Sandy, are you as depressed as Philip?

**Sandy**   If anything I'm slightly more depressed.

**Chief**   Hmm, I feel terrific.

**Sandy** (*after a tiny pause*)   I must say I'm perking up.

**Chief**   It seems to me, gentlemen, that what we are doing here is forgetting the Moon landings.

**Philip** (*mystified*)   Ahhhm, yes, Chief, you're right, I did leave the Moon landings out of this particular equation . . . was that terribly wrong of me?

**Chief**   The Moon landings were a financial disaster of horrendous proportions. Twenty billion dollars to achieve two small bags of dust; so much had been hoped of them; so little achieved; it would have been better if they had never even bothered. Until that is, somebody noticed the Velcro.

**Philip**   Velcro, Chief?

**Chief**    Millions of nylon hooks and eyes on fabric strips.

**Philip**    Uhm . . . yes, I know what it is, but . . .?

**Chief**    Developed for specific uses during the space programme, then somebody decided to stick it on anoraks and turned it into a Pot Noodle. Within fifty years it will have paid for the whole fiasco. Out of evil came forth good. Gentlemen, we must find new ways to use our machinery.

**Philip**    Uhm yes, forgive me, Sir, but it's *using* the machines that's the problem. I really am rather concerned that, well . . . we might have produced a product that might, well . . . kill someone.

**Sandy**    With all due respect to Philip, if the tobacco industry had taken that kind of line, some of the world's greatest sporting events would never have been sponsored.

**Chief**    No no, I think that Philip has a point, we certainly don't want deaths on our conscience, bad for morale, bad for business. However, a solution presents itself which also opens up a whole new world of commerce and profit.

**Philip**    It does?

**Chief**    It's really very simple . . . We build Super Suckers and Bumper Blowers, far in advance of anything currently available, and undertake to collect oxygen in under-populated areas. Then councils who find their atmospheres temporarily thinned, through, I might add, the actions of their own citizens, will be in a position to make up the shortfall by hiring us to pump some back into the public arena.

**Sandy**    My God! It's brilliant.

**Philip**   So, Chief, you're suggesting that having made
a huge profit from machines by which people hoard
oxygen, we now build bigger versions of the same
machines, in order to make further profits replacing it.

**Chief**   Exactly.

**Philip**   Look, Chief, call me an insanely cautious old
turd if you will; look me in the eye and say 'Phil, if you
drag your feet any further you're going to be tripping
over *tube* trains'; ring my people and tell them that their
boss wouldn't recognize solid gold if he was surrounded
by three quarters of a million Californians jumping up
and down, waving their pickaxes and shouting 'yeeha,
we've struck it', I just feel that there's going to be
objections.

**Chief**   Philip, we didn't create this situation, we only
make the machines. If a problem exists, the consumer
has created it and thank God we live in a society where
the consumer has a right to create problems.

**Philip** (*still doubtful*)   Yes, I see that certainly, it's just
that, well . . . selling air? I see a media backlash, and
frankly, I'm buggered if perhaps they wouldn't have a
point. I mean, everybody owns the air, don't they? We
don't really have a right to sell it? Do we? Or what?

**Chief** (*a tiny bit angrily*)   Yes, Philip, and while you're
taking your Ph.D. in moral semantics, Mr Suzuki is
laying down the keel of the first Super Sucker. You're
my top man, Philip, President of the division and quite
frankly I'm surprised . . .

**Sandy** (*pleased*)   Perhaps you're tired, Phil. You drive
yourself like an insane man.

**Chief**   The air is a natural resource. Like food or coal.
Is the grocer or the coal man wrong for selling his

wares? And yet people need food and warmth as much
as they need air. It seems that a man is to be allowed to
put bread on his table, clothes on the backs of his
children, buy land upon which they can run and play,
and yet he is to be denied the chance to provide fully
and properly for his family the most basic human
prerequisite of the lot, the wherewithal to breathe.
Denied that chance for fear that some hypothetical,
free-loading drop-out may find himself momentarily
short of breath.

**Sandy**    Phil, this is more than a business venture, it's a
moral crusade!

**Philip**    You're right, Sandy . . . sorry, Chief, just
thinking things through, that's all.

**Chief**    I understand, my boy . . . A fellow's always a
bit soft and loopy when he's in love, eh? Any
developments on that front yet? Can't have you
mooning about for ever.

**Philip**    Well, she did say something quite encouraging
a month or two back . . . haven't quite got round to
acting on it yet.

**Chief**    Ha ha, well, you get on with it, lad. Got to
clear the air, my boy. So that we can sell it.

# Act Two

### Scene One

*The control room of a huge air supplier.*

*There are consoles of buttons and flashing lights, computer screens, electronic maps of Britain with different coloured areas and arrows on them that could mean wind direction. If possible the arrows should move and the lights flash etc. There is celebration bunting hanging about, the Lockheart logo is very prominent, there is a dais and a ribbon to be cut, a table full of champagne. It is clearly a media opening.*

**Philip**, *in dinner jacket, is alone.*

**Philip** (*nervously rehearsing a speech*)   . . . It's just that what you said to me that time at Image Control . . . deeply sensible of enormous honour, yes deeply . . . Oh God, oh God . . . Come *on*, Philip, be a man, for Christ's sake, she's damn *hot* for you too, so just go for it!

**Kirsten** *enters, also dressed for the launch.*

**Kirsten**   Go for what, Philip?

**Philip** (*confused*)   What? Oh, just all this, Kirsty, you've really gone for it, no woman could do more, a truly Herculean effort. Christ, I don't think I've ever *seen* so much champagne and dippy things.

**Kirsten** (*checking things*)   Well, Philip, I can't deny I'm confident; the industry awards for the most champagne and dippy things at a launch are next month and I think our only real competition will be the first night of *Aspects of Mussolini*. I was very worried about last week's Channel Four re-re-relaunch but they blew it by switching to Asti Spumante after Michael Grade left.

**Philip** (*looking about*)    This launch is terribly important to me, Kirsty, it's a hearts and minds launch.

**Kirsten**    Which is why it's so important to get the champagne and dippy things right . . . Top quality bite-sized savoury thingies and plenty of them. (*She motions to a table.*) The times I've heard high-level opinion-formers dismiss an entire product range on the strength of soggy filo pastry.

**Philip**    Well, this little lot should guarantee some decent coverage.

**Kirsten**    You can never, never tell . . . you can have the most successful launch of all time, then Madonna gets out of a low slung sports car, some hack gets a decent shot of her knickers and you'll be lucky if the press find room for you on the sports pages.

**Philip**    It just goes to show 'there ain't no such thing as a free lunch'.

**Kirsten** (*slightly offended*)    Well, there isn't any call for that kind of comment.

**Philip** (*confused*)    What? I mean, did I . . . ?

**Kirsten** (*a zealot on her pet subject*)    Free lunch is what keeps the mighty cogs of public relations turning. Why, without free lunch there would be no more magazines, no more pop records, no more television programmes, no new estate agents opened . . .

**Philip**    God, heaven forbid.

**Kirsten**    Free lunch is the universal lubricant . . . from a tiny, two-person, tax-deductible power pasta to a six-hundred-head media faceful like this. Without free food, London would stop moving, we'd be a third world country in a month.

**Philip**   You're absolutely right, Kirsty, sorry . . . A fellow gets so tied up in his own little area that it's shamefully easy to forget the quite incredible amount of dedicated eating that has to go on just to bring a product before the public.

**Kirsten**   PR and Media *is* the product, Philip. As you say, it's hearts and minds.

**Philip**   Yes, no more so than in this case. Sadly, there are still people who rather resent their councils having to buy in private air to make the streets safe. We've got to get people to understand that pushing private air into the public arena is the inevitable result of people's God-given right to own their own air.

**Kirsten**   The press packs are very clear. (*She picks up a glossy brochure.*) I've had my very best people working on the buzz words and catch phrases . . . (*She flicks through.*) I'm particularly pleased with 'air's fair', and 'an Englishman's nose is his castle' . . . (*She looks at her watch.*) Christ, is that the time! Sir Chiffley will be here any moment, and I haven't checked that the waitresses' little black skirts are short enough . . . (*She makes to leave.*)

**Philip**   (*slightly embarrassed, grabbing his moment*)   Uhm, hang on a moment, Kirsten . . . there was something I wanted to say . . .

**Kirsten**   Better make it quick, Phil . . .

**Philip**   What? Oh yes, of course . . . well, it's just that . . . Oh hell, I'm not much good at this sort of thing . . . I wanted to tell you that you have got the most fantastic . . . most fantastic . . . people . . . No really, you have great . . . people and . . . and well . . . I'd really like to get my hands on them . . .

**Kirsten**   Thanks, Philip, I'll memo them.

**Philip**   I'd like to memo them too, Kirsten. Yes I
would, I'd like to give them a bloody good memo-ing, I
mean it . . . and it's not just your . . . people . . . I also
love your presentation, you have beautiful
presentation . . . You're a very special lady, Kirsten . . .

**Kirsten**   What's on your mind, Phil, is there a
problem?

**Philip**   Problem? A hundred and twelve types of 'no
way'! It's just, it's just that, well . . . Oh, this is
ridiculous, I don't need to be embarrassed, after all, I
know how *you* feel.

**Kirsten**   You do?

**Philip**   Yes, of course I do . . . after what you said in
the office that day, about the tasty elephant with G-spots
on his geezer . . .

**Kirsten**   Oh . . . you remembered.

**Philip**   Of course I remembered, Kirsty-wirsty. Christ
I'm young, Christ I'm romantic, Christ I'm a tasty
elephant . . . The world's beautiful and so are we . . .
And, I want you to know that it's all right . . . I feel the
same way.

**Kirsten**   You do?

**Philip**   Yes! Isn't that marvellous! It's like it was meant
to happen. *You* feel it, *I* feel it . . . we're already a team.

**Kirsten** (*very cold*)   I'm sorry, Philip, there's no way it
will work. Yes, all right, I admit what I feel, why
shouldn't I? But I had no idea you felt it too; honestly, if
I'd thought for a moment that we both felt the same way
then I would never have started this damn thing.

**Philip**   Christ, you girls don't half make it difficult!
Look, pretty speeches aren't normally my line, but I

really do think you're one *hell* of a bit of skirt, top-notch totty, senior bint etc., and any *normal* guy would have to be blind not to develop a major *horn* for you.

**Kirsten**    Philip, trying to flatter me isn't going to change anything, if you know how I feel you should understand that.

**Philip**    Of course I know how you feel, I know you're *hot* for the top stallion in the Lockheart stables, and I'm ready and willing to take the jumps with you!!

**Kirsten**    Right, that's enough! Just shut up right now! It's disgusting. I had no idea you felt this way, but let me tell you I'm not sharing Sandy with you, and if you two are planning some kind of dirty little AC/DC three-up sex game, count me out!

**Philip**    Oh come on, baby, why don't you just drop the pretence, drop the inhibitions, drop your pantyhose and let's do it!! Sharing Sandy? What . . . what do you mean?

**Kirsten**    You said you feel the same way I do; well, if you fancy Sandy, go for it, mate, but don't expect me along for the ride.

**Philip**    Uhm . . . look, I think there's a chance I may have dropped something of a clanger here . . . That day in your office, when you were bowling hints that there was a hot, hunky guy at Lockheart and you wanted in . . . you were . . . referring to Sandy?

**Kirsten**    Yes, I've liked him since that first day at my office. I thought you knew. I talked about him half the evening that night we went to dinner. I virtually never see him so I was hoping that you might drop a hint in the right direction . . . Hang on . . . Oh God, this is funny, you didn't . . . you didn't think that I fancied *you*?

**Philip**   Oh no! Not at all . . . well, yes, sort of . . .
anyway, ha ha, senior communication breakdown, eh?

**Kirsten**   I should say so. God, that is so funny!

**Philip**   You should have gone through your
people . . . or sent a fax . . .

**Kirsten**   I suppose it would have been simpler. Still,
no harm done, eh?

**Philip**   No, of course not . . . None whatsoever . . .
You really think it's funny, do you?

**Kirsten**   Of course, don't worry about it, I'm not
offended or anything, I just think it's an incredible joke,
don't you?

**Philip**   Of course, of course, of course. Ha ha.

*Fade to black-out.*

*A huge sob is heard.*

*Lights up, it is a little later,* **Sir Chiffley** *is at the podium,*
**Philip** *and* **Sandy** *respectfully flank him. All are in dinner
jackets.*

**Chief** (*making a speech*)   . . . Far in advance of any of our
competitors, Lockheart Air Division has completed this
major central distribution co-ordination master control
room . . . When it comes on line, this facility will be able
to access sufficient oxygen to waft the whole of Greater
London for up to twenty-eight days . . . The air industry
has come of age. At last we have a secure base from
which to serve the public . . . Now then, gentlemen,
ladies, I'm sure I've spoken enough and lunch is waiting.

*He steps down to polite taped applause.*

*The lights fade down. Immediately, taped sounds of a crowd eating
and chatting start up.*

*Lights up. It is a little later;* **Sir Chiffley** *is at the podium,* **Philip** *and* **Sandy** *respectfully flank him.*

(*Making a speech.*) . . . and so the doctor said 'Big breaths, Marjorie' and Majorie replied 'Yeth doctor and I'm only thixteen' . . . (*After a small laugh.*) Now, of course, there is in fact a very serious point to that story. For without the facilities that Lockheart Air Division can offer, facilities like this Central London Wafter which Lady Olga has so kindly opened for us – a wafter far in advance of anything our competitors are currently providing – without that, no doctor would feel confident in ordering a patient to take 'big breaths'. Rather, he would be obliged to say 'tiny pants, Marjorie', which, let's face it, quite apart from being totally inadequate on health grounds, would be a completely different joke. So there you are, then, I think I've made my point, and now gentlemen, ladies, lunch is waiting.

*The lights fade down and soon come up again: the event is over, tables are an empty mess, etc.* **Sandy** *and* **Philip** *are with* **Chief** *bow ties a bit undone, etc.* **Philip** *is slightly pissed.*

**Philip**    Well, Chief, a splendid speech, and a splendid launch in general . . . very inspiring . . . I feel great. I really do.

**Sandy**    Yes, marvellous, Chief, gives one a terrific glow. Mind you, we . . .

**Philip** (*rudely interrupting him*)    Yes, Chief, it's certainly a wonderful facility.

**Sandy** (*ignoring* **Philip**)    We could have done without the press going on and on about how much actual oxygen is getting through to the consumer . . .

**Chief**    I share their concern, Sandy, it's the classic problem of over-production. All the franchise holders have been sucking away like a hyperactive rent boy, and now the UK's been semi-sucked out and we're all sitting on huge tanks of compressed oxygen.

**Sandy**    Everyone's undercutting. (*He motions to areas flashing on the maps.*) It's beginning to look like a full-scale price war, Sir.

**Philip** (*aside to* **Sandy**)    Yes, all right, just pack in the leering innuendo bit, OK? You can have her, I don't give a toss. (*Back to* **Chief**.) It isn't so much the price I'm concerned about, Chief, it's more that not enough air is actually being wafted to the breathing public.

**Chief**    Well, we can't very well waft it until we've agreed a decent price for it, can we? Or what's the point of sucking it in the first place? We just have to get together with the other franchise holders and establish a stable minimum price. Good Lord, if a bunch of wops with dishtowels on their heads can establish an oil cartel, I think we should be just about able to set a decent price for a gulp of air.

**Sandy**    Well, I hope you're right, Chief, things are very unstable at the moment. We've seen green stamps, air miles, royal crested teaspoons, sherry schooners. It's insane! Do they really want to have to fight a free gift war? That's the kind of war nobody wins.

**Philip** (*waspish*)    Oh God, state the obvious, why don't you, Sandy. Sorry, Chief, I think his mind's on other things!

*Nobody really knows how to react.*

**Chief**    A free gift war would be a nightmare, we all know very well that free gift wars lead to shooting wars and by heaven I shan't allow hot-headedness of that sort to ruin this industry. Look what's happened in France,

organized crime, protection rackets. Thank goodness
the process leaves the atmosphere non-volatile so, within
limits, it is possible to administer an area on a regional
basis.

**Sandy**    Apart, of course, from the wind.

**Philip** (*still waspish*)    Yes, well, we all know that.

**Sandy**    Only two days ago in Hounslow, Essex, we're
scheduled to top up twelve thousand houses, plus the
council is taking delivery for its street wafting
obligations. Our boys are two miles out of town in a
twelve sucker convoy. What happens . . . the wind.

**Philip** (*unpleasantly imitating* **Sandy**)    'The wind'.

**Sandy** (*ignoring him*)    Suddenly everyone's jumping for
joy and stuffing their sucker tubes out of the window.

**Philip**    Well at least everybody got something to
breathe, I mean that's important too, isn't it? I mean,
fair's fair, the wind's the wind, after all.

**Sandy**    Philip, they were getting free air, where the
hell does that leave us?

**Chief**    No, Philip's right, the wind is the wind and I
see no reason why we cannot put it to our advantage,
most winds are fairly seasonal. It seems to me not an
unreasonable idea that we might anticipate the majority
of them.

**Philip** (*not understanding*)    Ye-es.

**Chief**    And send mobile suckers to the coast in order to
harvest the oxygen before the winds sweep inland. That
way the basic minimum gulp price will be protected and
the legitimate consumer will be protected from cowboys.

**Philip**    Well, of course, we have to protect the
consumer.

**Sandy**    The needs of the customer must come first.

**Philip**    I just *said* that, Sandy.

### Scene Two

*A* **TV Weather Woman** *comes on and stands by a map with her little cloud and rain stickers. She tries to be jokey in a farty, weedy way.*

**Weather Woman**    Well, I certainly hope some of you were enjoying the beautiful sunshine we've been experiencing in the South East. I know my roses were pretty pleased to see me . . . I'll tell you what . . . I don't know about talking to plants, but if my roses could talk to me, I expect they'd say, uhm . . . 'Where have you been, darling, don't see much of you' and 'what about these greenfly?' Ha ha. Anyway, moving on to tomorrow's weather; well, the most exciting thing is some very strong winds coming in over the Bristol Channel. Now these will be fresh in from the Atlantic and so they're likely to be completely full. Really brisk, lovely, oxygen-saturated winds, so why not get the Suck and Blow in the car and go and pick a few breaths up for nothing . . . make a family picnic of it.

Now a word of warning, there will also be strong gusting in the North West, but please don't get excited, that one's in from Scandinavia, and I'm afraid it will have been well and truly milked by the Swedes. Of course, it may have picked up something over the North Sea, but I should leave that one to the professionals, if I were you. Personally, I'll be sticking with my roses . . . ha ha, don't want them whispering about me behind my back. Ha ha ha. Good night.

## Scene Three

**Kirsten**'s *flat.*

**Kirsten** *and* **Sandy** *have just hosted a dinner party. She is at the door seeing out guests who we do not see.*

**Kirsten**   It was lovely to see you, Geoff, Christ knows when was the last time I got a bit pissed. Thanks for the lovely Shiraz by the way, I *love* Australian wine, it always walks away with the blind tastings . . . Anyway, it's been absolutely great, see you again soon . . . mmm, wonderful, bye . . . bye . . . (*She closes the door and walks back in.*) *God*, that bloody bloke can *breathe*!

**Sandy**   What?

**Kirsten**   I could not *believe* it! Could you believe it? I couldn't. I mean it's not necessary, is it? Sitting there like some great vacuum cleaner *sucking* in great gusts of the stuff. The man must have lungs like Zeppelins.

**Sandy**   Seemed perfectly normal to me.

**Kirsten**   I'm sure he could discipline himself to take smaller breaths, I mean it's just *rude*, it's not as if the stuff grows on trees. Next time I think I shall *have* to say something, just a little joke like 'coo, mind you don't suck up the sofa'. I mean, it is unbelievable, don't you think . . . ?

**Sandy**   Oh come on, Kirsten, he's an active bloke, I mean he has to breathe. Anyway, you didn't have to stand with the door open saying goodbye, did you?

**Kirsten**   Sandy, may I remind you that this is my bloody house, for which I work bloody hard and if I wish to stand with the bloody door open I shall bloody well do so!

**Sandy**    I'm just saying that if you're so worried about your air it's not your job to supply the whole street. You could have said goodbye with the door closed, you know.

**Kirsten**    Sandy, working in creative marketing may not be quite as lucrative as being golden boy to Sir Chiffley Lockheart, but I think I can just about afford sufficient oxygen to open my front door occasionally.

**Sandy**    Well, what's the problem then?

**Kirsten**    There isn't a problem! It's just the principle of the thing, I just find grunters and honkers incredibly antisocial that's all . . . and when he laughs!! Great pnematic snorts, just oxygenating the blood for no better reason than to grunt like a pig.

**Sandy**    He was laughing at my Stuttgart story, which, as it happens, I told bloody well.

**Kirsten**    I wouldn't mind but I was blowing some really terrific stuff tonight, Sicilian, sucked on the North face of Mount Etna, completely wasted on him, of course.

**Sandy**    Oh, for God's sake, I hope you're not turning into a real air snob, I can't stand real air snobs, going on and on about this bloody air and that bloody air, it's all bloody air to me.

**Kirsten**    I don't believe this! I simply do not *believe* this! Who's been talking about nothing but air all evening!

**Sandy**    Well, it's a bloody worrying time. There's a real free-trade backlash on the UK fixed-minimum gulp price, bloody Yank consortiums lobbying to bring in cheap air from bloody Africa, our stocks will be worthless . . .

**Kirsten**   I know, you haven't shut up about it for weeks!

**Sandy**   It's the bloody EEC. They *have* to subsidize European suckers, they're quite happy to subsidize wine lakes and butter mountains. The air industry's every bit as important to the European economy as farming, we must have air . . . (*He searches for the word.*) bubbles.

**Kirsten**   Look, can't we shut up about it for one night?

**Sandy** (*getting up and grabbing his coat*)   Well, if I'm being that dull, perhaps I should just piss off then?

**Kirsten**   Perhaps you should!

**Sandy**   Right . . . (*At the door.*) Would you object *terribly* if I took a final big gulp? My car's a good fifty yards away and your local council wafts at criminal levels.

**Kirsten**   Oh, for God's sake, Sandy, this is ridiculous.

**Sandy**   What?

**Kirsten**   I've been waiting for Geoff to go all evening so you could give me a right bloody seeing to, and now we're having a row.

**Sandy**   Well, I'm sorry, darling . . . you know, pressure etc . . .

**Kirsten**   I'm sorry too . . .

**Sandy** (*going to her*)   Come here, you ravishingly all right bit of grappling fodder you . . .

**Kirsten**   Hang on, I'll just change the balloon on the Suck and Blow; if we're going to be thrashing and groaning and just having a ruddy good bonk there's no point doing it to best Sicilian . . .

*The lights fade out as jets of steam shoot across the stage.*

## Scene Four

**Chief** and **Philip**, *towels round waists, having steam.*

**Chief** (*pouring water on a brazier of coals, provoking a great waft of steam*)    Do you know, Philip, I've been enveloped in most things in my time, from a woman's arms to a bathful of raw mackerel, and I still say there's nothing quite like the searing, cleansing heat of the steam-room to brace a fellow up.

**Philip** (*slightly preoccupied*)    Uhm, no, absolutely, Sir, senior searing.

**Chief**    I must say I do sometimes allow myself a wry smile when I hear it suggested that people like you and I don't know what it's like to really sweat. I mean, look at us now, positively evaporating. I shouldn't think a coal miner would last much above five minutes in here.

**Philip** (*still preoccupied, not really listening*)    Absolutely not, Chief, we'd have the grimy blighter thrown out pretty sharp.

**Chief**    All right, young fellow, what's stuck in your craw? Is it that girl from marketing? Getting serious, is she?

**Philip**    Chief, that's history, I walked, I was out of there. I said to her, I said 'Listen lady, I'm dust, I'm a memory, don't look for me tomorrow, baby, because I'll be long gone'.

**Chief**    And what did she say?

**Philip**    She said 'all right', which I respected her for.

**Chief**    Do you know, Philip, I've always seen it as rather a mistake to respect a woman, they see it as a sign of weakness.

**Philip**    We nearly had it all, Chief, we were perfect for one another, everything was right, except for the fact that she wasn't interested in me. That was the real problem and I just had no time to deal with that.

**Chief**    How could you have, Philip? Your life's a Pot Noodle now. Look laddie, I've seen women every shape and every colour, but I've never met one yet who had a first-year turnover in excess of twenty billion. (*He puts more water on the steaming coals.*)

**Philip**    Mmm, yes, it's rather this Pot Noodle business that's been preoccupying me during our executive steam, Chief, and making me perhaps slightly less charismatic company than I might have hoped. (*He puts more water on the steaming coals. After a pause.*) Chief, I wonder if you'd mind if I showed you something that's rather worrying me.

**Chief** (*worried*)    Well, I don't know, Philip, I'm not a doctor. I do know a fellow in Kensington who's very discreet . . .

**Philip**    I've been sent this letter. (*He fishes out a letter from under his towel.*) It's got rather soggy, I'm afraid . . .

**Chief**    A letter, Philip?

**Philip**    Yes, Chief, it's a kind of fax but there's no telephone lines involved. It inputs via a slit in the door, terrific concept . . .

**Chief**    I know what a letter is, Philip. I'm constantly receiving them from some people called 'Freeman's Catalogue', apparently with their help I could look as good as Lulu. I confess I've always found Lulu extremely attractive, but then I find trees attractive and I wouldn't want to look like a tree, would I? So where's the logic in that? Anyway, what's so special about your soggy one? Do we have a legal problem?

**Philip**   It's the reply that the American Indian Chief, known as Seattle, sent in eighteen fifty-four to the US Government on receipt of their request to buy from him the land of his people.

**Chief**   You've been sent a letter by a dead Red Indian?

**Philip**   No, Chief, someone has anonymously sent me a copy of the dead Chief's letter and it has moved me, Sir. I could not have been more moved if I had been reading it on Concorde.

**Chief**   Sounds like potent stuff.

**Philip**   I truly believe that I would scarcely have been as emotionally affected by the contents of this letter if they had been written on a Stinger ground-to-air missile and fired up my trouser leg.

**Chief**   Strong reaction, Philip. Tell me more.

**Philip**   Well, as I say, it concerns this old tomahawk-twirling scalp collector named Seattle, who seems to have carried senior executive status over a predominantly hunter-gathering workforce operating out of Northern California in the middle of the last century.

**Chief**   Go on.

**Philip**   Well, as I explained, he was memo-ing Washington *vis-à-vis* their purchase offer on certain choice properties of Red Indian real estate . . . Now this is his answer . . . (*He reads.*) 'Every part of the earth is sacred to my people' . . . Amazing how little changes in corporate structuring, eh, Sir Chiffley? This fellow Seattle had his people just as you or I do . . .

**Chief**  The first rule of the jungle, Philip, is to know how to delegate.

**Philip**  Every time, Chief, and if you're too busy to delegate yourself then for God's sake get someone to do it for you.

**Chief**  Delegate, delegate, delegate. Wasn't it John Lennon who sang 'power to the people'?

**Philip**  Becoming the only major star in the history of rock to write a song about delegation within a management structure . . .

**Chief**  Small wonder the world remembers him.

**Philip**  Well, quite. Anyway, as I was saying, Seattle has talked to his people and they have made a policy decision that (*He refers to the letter.*) 'Every part of the earth is sacred' . . . and now he is memo-ing the US Government on the issue. He continues . . . (*He reads.*) 'Every shining pine needle, every sandy shore, every mist in the dark woods, every clearing and humming insect is holy in the memory and experience of my people' . . .

**Chief**  Holy insects?

**Philip**  Gripping stuff, eh? (*He reads.*) 'We know that the white man doesn't understand our ways. One portion of land is the same to him as the next for he is a stranger who comes in the night and takes from the land whatever he needs. The Earth is not his brother but his enemy' . . .

**Chief**  I must confess, Philip, I have little patience with this fellow so far. The earth isn't a man's brother or his enemy, it's just the earth, I'm afraid.

**Philip**  Oh, I think it's more complicated than that, Sir, hear him out, you'll find it's worth it... (*He reads.*)

'The sight of your cities pains the eyes of the Red man. There is no quiet place, no place to hear the unfurling of the leaves in Spring or the rustle of the insects' wings' . . .

**Chief**   I can't say as how I've ever heard a leaf unfurl, have you, Philip?

**Philip**   Incredibly acute hearing these Redskins, Chief. Just by putting their ears to the ground they could say how many riders were coming, how heavily they were armed and what they'd all had for dinner. Hearing leaves would have been junior stuff to them. Anyway, Seattle sticks with the theme . . . (*He carries on reading.*) 'The clatter of your cities insults our ears, and what is there to life if a man cannot hear the lonely cry of the whippoorwill or the arguments of the frogs around a pond at night? If we sell you our land, you must keep it apart and sacred as a place where even the white man can go to taste the wind that is sweetened by the meadow's flowers' . . .

**Chief**   In which case there wouldn't be an awful lot of point in buying it, would there? Look, Philip, I'm sorry, but I simply don't see the relevance of all this to the air industry.

**Philip** (*pacing about*)   Well, Sir, as I originally saw it, the real excitement of our sucking operations was that we had found a way to tame the final element for the good of mankind, just as food and power and water and the very land itself had once been tamed.

**Chief**   Well, I think that's a fair, if perhaps rather fanciful way of describing raking in a wadge of cash.

**Philip**   Then, when people started wandering around going purple and gasping for breath I thought, 'Whoops, hang on, hullo . . . I wasn't under the impression that going purple and gasping for breath was particularly high up on the list of things that are for the good of mankind' . . . It struck me that it wasn't awfully long since everybody had had enough to breathe, and now, bugger me, but for the good of mankind, they hadn't any more . . . I mean, old Seattle saw it coming with the land . . .

**Chief**  My dear Philip, I'm sure you'll forgive me, but this fellow Seattle strikes me as being a bit of a turd. Throughout history there has always been some environmental luddite standing in the way of the natural development of a free-market economy.

**Philip**  Yes, but . . .

**Chief**  If the United States legislature had so far shirked their responsibilities as to listen to this Seattle fellow where would the world's greatest democracy be now? Sniffing wind, listening to leaves and having arguments with the frogs, that's where.

**Philip**  You're right, of course, Chief . . . I just thought it might form the basis for a memo on policy development . . . After all, we do want our industry to be a valuable part of society, don't we?

**Chief**  Of course we do, Philip, as valuable as it can possibly be, but there's only so much we can do to force up the price . . .

*Steam.*

You know Philip, I've been doing a bit of thinking as well.

**Philip**  Nothing like it, eh?

**Chief**  Philip, you're my best man and I'm going to be perfectly straight. I think you're tired, you've headed up the whole operation from the beginning and you deserve a break. I want you to take a break, so what do you say? Change of air?

**Philip**   I can get that at the chemist, Sir.

**Chief**   I want you to take some leave, Philip.

**Philip**   Well, I suppose . . . I don't know . . . I just hate to see people go breathless, that's all.

**Chief**   Philip, it's a small portion of the population, the vast majority are breathing cleaner, healthier air . . . besides, the whole thing is a political issue. It has nothing to do with us, we just provide a service.

*Steam fills the stage.*

**Scene Five**

*The steam clears.*

*The **Minister for the Environment** is making a speech.*

**Minister**   Of course we recognize that there is suffering and we will continue to seek out the truly deserving cases and provide them with all the help that they require . . . However, we believe that the onus lies partly with the less well off themselves to alleviate the problem. As with poor diet, we believe the main enemy is ignorance. In nineteen eighty-eight the Government issued detailed advice to the hungry on how best to gain sustenance. They advised in a leaflet issued through the Department of Health and Social Security that people should avoid treats and impulse buys, that they should not go shopping for food when they were hungry since this would lead them into unwise purchases. I feel that similar common-sense measures will help the less well off

with their breathing. The plain facts are that some
people are simply not breathing properly. For
instance, is it really necessary for people to breathe
quite so much? If you find yourselves in difficulties,
surely it would be possible to take shorter breaths. In
the home, if your income requires you to have your
blower on minimal output, try to move about less;
silly and wasted movements just use up precious
energy . . . Lie down on your bed and take slow,
well-spaced breaths . . . perhaps you could time
them. Avoid activities that you know will consume
air, keep family discussion to a minimum, don't go
upstairs if you can possibly avoid it, the lavatory is a
key danger, go only when you know it's coming, any
straining will throw your meter sky high. Obviously
love making is a very irresponsible activity when
the air is thin, definitely to be avoided. Ask
Grandma not to knit so vigorously and get rid of the
dog . . .

*His voice is drowned by the roar of a jet.*


**Scene Six**

*Huge jet engine noises.*

**Kirsten** *and* **Sandy** *are down stage in two business-class
British Airways seats.*

**Sandy**   Well, darling, what could be more perfect, a
combined honeymoon and business trip.

**Kirsten**   I couldn't believe it when Chief gave me the
International Portfolio.

**Sandy**   Kirsten, the Chief knows I don't marry
turkeys . . .

**Kirsten**    And he knows I don't marry men who marry turkeys.

**Sandy**    *Touché* Lady . . . tell you what, five hours fingering my laptop's put a right ruddy firework in my jocks. (*He puts the laptop down.*) What say we bog up and join the Five Mile High Club?

**Kirsten**    Been there, Sandy; believe me, there just isn't room. I was eighteen, doing Europe, ended up with some Frenchman having to prise me off one of the taps. Maybe if your secretary had put us in first . . .

**Sandy**    Yes, well, she won't make that mistake again.

**Kirsten**    Good.

**Sandy**    No chance, I sacked her by fax from Heathrow. But either way, first or business, flying is just a chore to me. I've cloud-hopped a deal too many flights to be spending my time saying, 'Oh, look how clever, they've managed to get the cod mornay and the strawberry cream dessert into the same container'.

**Kirsten**    Absolutely; anyway, it will be the best of everything for us once we clinch the African deal. Lucky for us Philip took leave, or he'd be heading it up.

**Sandy**    Luck, darling? Twelve types of hardly. The guy needed a break. Some people bend, some people snap, personally I'm a bender.

**Kirsten**    He had a good dream.

**Sandy** (*looking out of the window*)    Well, it's certainly going to come true for these African fellahs, I reckon they'll strike a hard bargain. They've got a phenomenal natural resource just waiting to be sucked; I mean, it'll be worth billions to their economy. The Chief's told me to bid top dollar. Incoming Third World air could totally undercut European stockpiles.

*His phone rings.*

Sorry, darling, it's the new Foton Satellite System, quite
superb . . . (*He takes out the portable.*) Yo, Chief!! Well, this
is a pleasure, Sir . . . (*He adjusts his tie.*) Marvellous,
Sir . . . What? Uhm, cod mornay and strawberry cream
dessert . . . Yes, it is clever how they do that, isn't it . . .
sorry? With all due respect, Sir . . . (*To* **Kirsten**.) Pen,
pen, pen . . . (*Into the phone.*) Fire away, Sir . . . (*He takes
down something.*) Right you are, Sir . . . What? Sadly no,
Sir, Kirsten says the taps get in the way . . . Goodbye
then, Sir . . . Kind regards to Lady Chiffley . . . (*He
switches the phone off.*) Sod it.

**Kirsten**    So what was that about?

**Sandy**    Said he thought I might need Philip's advice
on the African suck-up . . . gave me the bloke's bloody
number on the Costa Del Lager Lout . . . Well, that's
what I think of that! (*He screws up the paper, is about to throw
away, then slips in his pocket.*)

**Kirsten**    Bloody cheek . . .

*Film flicker effect.*

Oh God, the bloody awful movie . . .

**Sandy**    *Crocodile Dundee Four*, this is the one where he
becomes President of the Soviet Union . . . It's great . . .

*Plane noise fades off and the lights on* **Kirsten** *and* **Sandy**
*fade down.*

*Lights come up on* **Philip** *on one side of the stage, in shorts and a
sombrero. He takes a sip of wine and clicks a TV remote . . .
There is a very low bluish flicker, as if he is watching TV.*

**Scene Seven**

*We hear a terrible buzzing of flies, people wailing, oxen snorting.*

*A BBC* **Reporter** *with a microphone wanders across front of stage. She has a backpack which feeds a tube to a big plastic bubble on her head.*

**Reporter**    These people are quite literally suffocating. The air is so thin that they find it difficult to find the energy to move . . . (*She appears to pick her way over something.*) Of course, there was a time when this region possessed oxygen in abundance. It still would have, were it not for the fact that the rulers of this tortured, divided country, both on the left and right, have systematically sold its resources for arms. Western developers, with the connivance of a corrupt administration, have sucked far beyond agreed international quotas. Now this region is all but uninhabitable. (*She stops wandering about.*) While this tiny child gulps painfully at the near empty and useless air, the oxygen that should be her rightful birthright lies unbreathed, far far away, stockpiled in order to protect the international gulp price. That she should be in such desperate straits whilst the means for her survival lies silent, invisible, useless, compacted down into the huge Western Suck and Blowers, is vivid testimony of man's inhumanity to man. (*She stops again.*) This goat did not die naturally, it was slaughtered by the very people whose survival depends on its milk and meat. The need for air supersedes even the need for food and as the air thins, animals are slaughtered in order to stop them breathing and consuming what little oxygen remains. (*She motions around her.*) This relief camp, jointly run by Oxfam and War on Want, is currently supplying breathing space for about four and a half thousand refugees. They have struggled here, gasping for breath from their homes in the outlying hills where the air is now too thin for survival. The scene is biblical in its horror. The relief workers are operating three dilapidated Mark One Lockheart Blowers at the centre of the camp and people scramble desperately trying to find a place near one of the outlets for themselves and their children. The further away one is, of course, the less chance there is of a really good lungful. Added to this is the terrible uncertainty that a sudden gust of empty wind will carry off and dissipate the precious pumpings, leaving the entire camp momentarily without the means to live. Whenever even the slightest breeze is felt, a great moan goes up and people huddle closer, breathing deeply, bracing themselves for the possibility of two or three minutes with nothing to breathe at all . . . So far in this present crisis over four million people have been terminally suffocated or died from the associated problems of hunger and rioting . . . (*She addresses the imaginary cameraman, in a brisk professional tone.*) Did you get the baby in, Barry? The shot won't work without the baby.

*The* **Reporter** *wanders off.*


## Scene Eight

*A plastic tunnel stretches across the stage, the back half of it anyway; the front part is open for the audience to see in.*

**Sandy** *bustles on with the* **Chief**, *both wearing hard hats.*

**Sandy**    Sorry I was late, Chief, some bastard actually broke in and stole my air! Just whipped the balloon right off the sucker; I mean, Christ, that is sick! Bloody ironic as well, it must have happened while I was in the sitting-room watching the ITV Breathathon . . . To think while I was trying to get through to the credit card hotline to let a baby breathe, some bugger was actually taking the air from right under my nose.

**Chief**  Yes, Lady Chiffley doesn't feel safe outside any more, there's so many people on the streets hanging about breathing . . . Apparently they can't afford to waft their own homes so they stay out half the night breathing public air.

**Sandy**  We saw you on the Breathathon though, Sir, donating the Lockheart cheque; it was so great to see you with all those alternative comedians. Terrific for the company image. And so incredibly worthwhile. I couldn't believe it when they cut to that beautiful little Sudanese baby and said our cheque would keep fifty thousand like her breathing for a year. Kirsten cried . . .

**Chief**  Yes, well, it was a fun night and we're all proud to have done our bit to help, but we have work to do. How are we progressing with the breather tubes?

**Sandy**  Terrifically, Chief; as you can see, we're well on course. (*He motions round.*) The tubes are fashioned from a fully translucent plastic substitute; hence, while enjoying the air, the public user – be they a housewife going about her usual workaday routine, busy executive, or overseas visitor – they will be afforded an unrivalled view of the on-street features and the shopping opportunities available outside. (*He shows it all off.*)

**Chief**  Yes, well, I must say it looks very smart.

**Sandy**  Many thanks, Chief; my people are good, damn good, there isn't one of them that isn't being individually groomed. The secondary advantages of the Breather Tube system need, of course, no explanation, so if I can just explain them, they are in the areas of civic cleanliness, and the prevention of civic skin cancer –

**Chief**    Sandy, the advantage of these tubes is that if you are inside one you won't suffocate.

**Sandy**    I'm certain they're going to prove an enormous earner. With councils cutting back so heavily on the strength of their atmosphere, anyone who can possibly afford it will choose to use the Lockheart Oxygenated walkways. Entrance, as you can see, is facilitated by credit card, so if Access and Visa want in they'd better get ready for the pips to squeak . . .

**Chief**    Excellent. Excellent.

**Sandy**    Shops who want to be connected up to the tube will of course have to pay massive rental on their entrance . . .

**Chief**    And, of course, they'll all have to connect because any halfway decent customer is going to be in the first-class tubes . . .

**Sandy**    Uhm, actually, I was speaking to Kirsten about that term, Sir; she felt the term 'first-class' rather divisive and suggested the more user-friendly 'Alpine class'.

**Chief**    I was not aware we had anything to apologize for, Sandy.

**Sandy**    Well, either way, Sir, I think a major back-slapping session is in order, Chief; these tubes have definitely opened up another serious market for Lockheart Oxy.

**Chief** (*snapping*)    They haven't opened anything up! All they have done is managed to recoup a little of what we are losing through the neverending cut-backs in oxygen consumption that our industry faces every day . . .

**Sandy**    Yes, but –

**Chief**    There are no buts, just facts. We have developed these tubes in response to dizzy shoppers demanding breathable air at street level.

**Sandy**    Exactly, and –

**Chief**    And the reason that demand exists is because of Poll-Tax-capped councils cutting further and further back on the amount of oxygen they waft. Do you know what's going to happen next? I shall tell you: local councils are going to ask themselves, why if the private sector can enclose the environment can't they? They'll build their own civic walkways beside ours . . . The simple fact is that people are learning to live with much less air.

**Sandy**    Pretty chilling thought, Sir.

**Chief**    I remember young Philip saying that the party was over a few months before he went on leave. I hope the poor chap isn't proved right.

**Sandy**    The guy just couldn't take the pressure of down-swing, Sir.

**Chief**    The short-term solution is simple: we sell less air, but we charge more for it. I feel certain that the other members of the cartel will have no objections to raising the minimum gulp price. What happens in the long term we shall have to ponder, but believe me, there is a recession coming, and when it does, it will be a cruel wind that blows and it won't bring any of us any good.

*A huge wind is heard. The muffled crumps of explosions. The auditorium flickers orange with flames, interspersed with bright red-orange flashes.*

## Scene Nine

*The **Chief**'s office.*

*The huge windows glow red, suggesting enormous fires going on outside. Occasionally there is a hot flash followed by a muffled 'crump'. Obviously, the effect should be dramatic.*

*Perhaps there is a trolley of champagne.*

**Kirsten**, **Sandy**, *the* **Chief** *and* **Philip** (*possibly heavily sun-tanned.*)

**Chief**   Well now, Philip, my dear boy, it's splendid to have you back on side.

**Philip**   It's good to be back, Chief. I'm tanned, I'm fit, I'm raring like a rarerer.

**Chief**   I can't tell you how happy that makes me, you're my top man, you know that. Sandy's been heading up your presidency portfolio in your absence, but I know how delighted he'll be to hand the reigns back to you.

**Sandy** (*obviously not delighted*)   Delighted, Philip. It's a total pleasure . . .

**Chief**   Sandy's good, Philip, damn good, but I need creative thinking at the very top. Some people discover Pot Noodles, some people make sure that they're stacked neatly on shelves. I think Sandy understands the difference.

**Sandy** (*a bit taken aback*)   Well, I . . .

**Kirsten** (*defensively*)   Sir Chiffley, I don't think that's . . .

**Chief**   So tell me, Philip, you've been on the outside looking in for a while, what are your

impressions of the situation. Not idyllic by any means,
I imagine.

**Philip**    Chief, I'm a straight talking man, I'm not the
sort of person to beat up a bush or waste words on
mincers. The situation as I see it is serious.

**Sandy**    Yes, it's serious, Chief, but with major plant
closures –

**Kirsten**    Strategic lobbying, saturation mail-shots –

**Chief**    Shut up, Sandy, you too, Kirsten. Philip's right,
the whole industry has gone haywire, it's the nineteen
seventy-three oil glut crisis all over again. There is
simply too much bloody air around.

**Philip** (*surprised*)    Too *much* air, Chief? Difficult to see
that, I had to step over a couple of prostrate gaspers just
between the car and the office.

**Chief**    Exactly. People aren't breathing enough of the
bloody stuff. Philip, my boy, it would be as well if we
faced the facts squarely and like men. A combination of
huge stockpiles and massively decreased demand have
forced this great industry of ours into a vortex-like
recession. It's time to face the music. I'm afraid it's
going to be pretty unpleasant.

**Philip**    Bananarama time.

**Sandy**    Philip's right, of course, the situation is
bloody serious. Kirsten's been running background
makes on –

**Kirsten**    Yes, I've got Venn diagrams that will –

**Chief**    Young lady, when I'm up to my neck in shit I
don't need a graph to tell me how deep it is . . .

**Sandy** *laughs sycophantically.* **Kirsten** *shoots him an angry
look.*

There aren't many single industries big enough to create recessions that grow into full-scale depressions . . . oil, automobiles, dieting, cosmetic surgery in the States . . .

**Philip**    Phew! You're right there, Chief, I remember when Cher imploded. The whole industry collapsed. Let me tell you, when it comes to cosmetic surgery, if the bottom falls out, you might as well go home.

**Chief**    And likewise with air, Philip; if we go down, the rest follows.

**Philip**    Nice to be up there with the big ones, Chief. (*He crosses to the window.*) I must say this African oxygen doesn't half burn.

**Sandy**    It should burn, the price Kirsten and I paid for it.

**Kirsten**    We had a marvellous trip, Philip. I brought you back a Nobbuck made out of dried bark and berries. It rattles when you shake it.

**Philip**    Hmm, yes, actually I've been meaning to ask you about this, Chief. I mean, seeing as how it cost us so much and, well, seeing as how the world is positively seething with purple-faced gaspers, and I must stress here, Chief, *children* are involved . . . is it actually really one hundred per cent necessary to burn so much oxygen? I mean, really?

**Chief**    Philip, you know as well as I do that there is only one way to guarantee an adequate supply of oxygen and that is for the world to realize that if it wants to breathe it's going to have to accept reasonable pricing levels . . .

**Philip**    Hmm yes, but . . .

**Chief**    The only way we can hope to recoup some of

the cost of total world sucking is to force up the price, and the only way to do that is to rationalize stocks.

*Another huge glow and a 'grump' noise at the window.*

We can't sell the stuff, and having so much of it hanging around totally destabilizes the price . . .

**Philip** (*staring out of the window*)    I still can't help feeling somehow that people could have breathed that stuff . . .

**Sandy**    Philip's been away a while, Sir. I don't think he understands the new reality.

**Philip**    I think I'm looking at it, Sandy.

**Kirsten**    The whole effect will look great on my corporate video. It'll really gee up the sales force.

**Chief**    Have you any idea how much grain was destroyed in the eighties, Philip? While people starved, how much milk was poured away while babies screamed with want? Nobody likes it, Philip, but you can't just give the stuff away; that way lies financial anarchy.

**Philip**    I admire your strength of commitment, Chief. It would be so easy to make the obvious equation . . . People are suffocating: so burning oxygen is wrong. But you look further, you see the practical necessities of modern finance.

**Chief**    Somebody has to do it, Philip. Anyway, there is actually a very real upside to our present burning programme.

**Philip**    There is?

**Chief**    Oh, absolutely, now there's so little oxygen in the exterior atmosphere, obviously it's not possible to burn anything . . .

**Philip**    Yeah, they've just disbanded Britain's last fire brigade.

**Kirsten**    I got some super nostalgia spreads in the tabloids . . .

**Chief**    So we've been able to do a rather decent little deal with the EEC agricultural cartel selling them our oxygen to burn their crops with. Now *that's* the sort of sound economics and good husbandry that keeps the world turning.

**Philip** (*still at the window*)    So there's food besides air in these fires?

**Sandy**    Damn right there is, how else do you think agri-business is to maintain a fair price for its product?

**Philip** (*thoughtfully*)    The works of man upon earth, eh? They have an awesome and majestic beauty.

**Chief** (*joining him at the glowing windows, his arm on* **Philip***'s shoulder*)    God created nature, Philip, and man tamed it.

**Philip**    One hell of a partnership.

**Chief**    Yes, but we haven't completely tamed the old fellow yet, you know, He's still got a few tricks up His sleeve.

**Philip**    God?

**Chief**    Clever old sod. (*He holds up a test tube.*) Just take a look at this, Philip . . . it's green chlorophyll, the greatest enemy of the oxygen industry. This little natural vandal could, in time, destroy us and the jobs and revenue that we create.

**Philip**    Bugger me backwards, Chief, it hardly seems possible: it's so small, so insignificant.

**Chief**   Well, this isn't all of it, Philip, obviously.

**Philip**   Isn't it? Oh I see, yes, of course not, Chief.

**Chief**   But there's a dollop of this in every leaf. In this. (*He fingers the potted plants.*) And in this. Every bit of green is packed with the stuff, and every day, whenever the sun shines, it whittles away, undermining the very basis of our great industry, threatening to cancel out the carefully regulated stocks upon which the gulp price is calculated.

**Philip**   But this must be quite awesomely worrying for you, Chief.

**Chief**   It is, Philip. Jemina. Mopsy. Janet over there. They're not just old friends any more. They are business competitors. Now think of our motor industry; well, what would happen to it if nature started growing cars?

**Philip**   It would be knackered, Chief.

**Chief**   Exactly, the situation has simply got to be regulated or else it will become impossible to set a price or manage the industry. It is possible to chemically manufacture oxygen, I see no reason to allow nature to do it . . .

**Sandy**   We have a global defoliation programme all geared up and ready to go. We've tested the chemicals on over a million beagles, and the last one hundred thousand or so survived more or less intact, so that should shut up the environmentalists.

**Kirsten**   I've been working on the trade justification campaign for weeks.

**Chief**   Obviously we can't do it alone, it will take world co-operation, but if the oil and motor industries can conspire against the cheap clean electric car in order to protect their expensive, dirty product, and the light bulb industry can sit on the everlasting bulb –

**Philip**    Painful.

**Chief**    – I see no reason why we shouldn't clear up this chlorophyll pest . . . (*He snips the head off a potted plant.*) Tscch. Business is business . . .

**Philip**    Chief, sorry to interrupt you when you're on a roll, but I think it's time I cut right through the bull's doo doo. Forget green chlorophyll, forget burning food mountains, we've got problems so huge you couldn't fit them into an elephant's trousers. Now I have an idea, Chief, it's one I've been a-mulling for quite a time span. Interested?

**Chief** (*alert and interested*)    Philip, it's a fool who thinks he's nothing left to learn . . . A fellow might wake up one morning thinking he's seen everything, and then he accidentally squats over a mirror and surprises himself. What's on your mind?

**Philip**    Well, before I switch to explanation mode, Chief, there's a degree of corporate restructuring that I'd like to implement in my capacity as President of the Air Division.

**Chief**    Carry on, Philip.

**Philip** (*with his back to* **Kirsten** *perhaps taking an off-hand interest in some portfolio*)    Uhm yes, it appears that while I was away, we seem to have taken some rather expensive media wallahs on to the staff. I'm thinking particularly of the uhm . . . (*He checks a document.*) ah yes, the Kirsten girl from Image Control . . .

**Kirsten**    Philip!

**Philip**   Chief, I'm looking at shrinking demand, I'm looking at shrinking profit, this is a time for retrenchment, not reckless expansion, so I'm afraid we're going to have to let her go . . . (*He turns round.*) Kirsten, you're sacked.

**Kirsten**   Philip, I don't believe this, if this is just petty jealousy . . . !

**Philip**   Look, I don't have time for histrionics, lovey. Sir Chiffley and I have an entire air industry to turn round and frankly, pretty adverts just ain't going to get the job done. Your desk has been cleared, the magnetic on your security laminate has already been wiped. You're out, OK?

**Kirsten**   I don't deserve this, Philip . . .

**Chief**   Harsh stuff, Philip, I can't help feeling . . .

**Philip**   Chief, this is my Pot Noodle, I started it, I'm President of it and by buggery I'm going to build my team, with the people I want. Now if you have a problem with that, Chief, then fine, but there is no way I am telling you my brilliant new idea while that woman is in this room.

**Chief**   There's a new vigour to your staff relations, Philip, I like it. (*To* **Kirsten**.) Goodbye, we're all terrible sorry to see you go.

**Kirsten**   Sandy, say something!

**Philip**   Yes, come on, Sandy, say something. Which is it to be, the totty or the company? Don't dither.

**Sandy**   Uhm . . . I . . .. well . . .

*During the following,* **Kirsten** *moves to the door.*

**Philip**   Chief, that's the kind of dither span that could lose us upwards of a trillion yen on the floor in Tokyo.

Get out, Sandy, we'll discuss it later. Get out both of you; if I'm going to pull the Chief's irons out of the fire I don't need dead wood adding to the flames . . .

**Kirsten** *is at the door.*

Kirsten, I want you to remember this.

**Kirsten** *turns and looks, then turns on her heel and exits.*

**Sandy** *makes a mute appeal to the* **Chief**, *who shrugs and nods towards the door.*

**Sandy** *exits.*

**Chief**   Quite a scene, Philip. I hope your ideas justify the preamble.

**Philip**   Hope trade's pretty light on the international markets, Chief, I sell certainties . . . I've been looking at the whole downside on the Private Air initiative and I reckon I've come up with my best idea yet. I'm very excited, so excited in fact that I haven't even told my people, I've brought the whole caboodle straight to the top. This is very much a between ourselves initiative, Sir, we can take no risks of interference.

**Chief**   Now this really is exciting . . . (*He moves to the desk, brisk and excited, and hits buttons.*) Full security, if you'd be so kind, Miss Hodges, I believe we have a potential Pot Noodle in the building . . . (*He hits more buttons.*)

*The same security measures as in Act One happen: great metal screens on windows and doors etc. The flaming flickering and 'crumps' from outside are now shut out, the lights are as normal.*

All right, Philip, we have maximum security, and you have my maximum attention.

**Philip**   OK, Chief, as you know I've been pondering the world implications of our colossal Pot Noodle ever since the first pensioner turned purple?

**Chief**    Absolutely, and it does you credit, Philip, it's essential to keep your eye on what I believe is currently called the downside.

**Philip**    Always watch the ground, what profiteth it a man to look to the top of the mountain if he's got dog doo on his shoes. Anyway . . . for quite a while I was able to rationalize the major human-suffering downside of our industry . . . I accepted that some have more air than others, that profits have to be made . . . But I can't deny that I rather stuck on the mass suffocation bit.

**Chief**    But Philip, you've always been perfectly happy to live in a world that countenances mass starvation . . . mass homelessness . . .

**Philip**    Granted, Chief, senior good point. It's just whereas you saw the example of food and shelter as justifying our air activities . . . I've rather come to see the air example as telling us something about food and shelter.

**Chief**    Rather tortured logic, if I might say so, Philip. In fact I'm not altogether sure I follow it . . . Have you got an idea or haven't you?

**Philip** (*excited*)    Definitely, Chief, no seriously, it's a whopper, a real whale's love weapon . . . Let me take you through its base line development.

**Chief**    I would be delighted.

**Philip**    Well, I was looking at the suffering, the recession, the poverty, the suffocation that I had been a large part of causing . . . and I had this huge idea . . .

**Chief**    Yes!

**Philip**    I thought, 'I know, I'll kill myself'.

**Chief**    By which you mean?

**Philip**   Kill myself.

**Chief** (*after a pause*)   So it's not a metaphor? You actually mean, kill yourself, that's your idea?

**Philip**   Yes.

**Chief**   But for God's sake, Philip, what are you saying? How can you blame yourself, my boy, it was just good business, that's all, you're being stupid, foolish . . .

**Philip**   Well, yes, I must admit that after a bit that's what I thought as well, Chief.

**Chief**   I'm extremely pleased to hear it.

**Philip**   So I thought it would be better to kill you.

**Chief**   What!

**Philip**   But then I thought, come *on*, Phil, this is a brainstorming ideas session, let's apply some Larry Logic . . . no point in killing the Chief, I thought, that would be absurd . . .

**Chief**   Good, excellent thought.

**Philip**   He's just one of many . . .

**Chief**   Well, quite.

**Philip**   I should kill them all . . .

**Chief**   Now look, Philip, please, for goodness sake . . .!

**Philip**   No, hang on, Chief, let me stage-by-stage you on this one . . . Next I thought, this is just ridiculous, I can't possibly go and kill all the people who profit out of suffering . . . it would be impossible: in a way, we all do.

**Chief**   Of course, of course, thank heavens you've . . .

**Philip**   So I went back to the idea of just killing you.

**Chief** (*after a pause*)    Yes, and what did you think then?

**Philip**    Nothing, I stopped there, that's it, that's my idea.

**Chief**    But . . . but . . . you just said yourself it would be pointless . . . !

**Philip**    I know, but I still think it's a good idea, even besides that.

**Chief** (*hitting the intercom*)    Security! Emergency . . .

*But the intercom is useless.*

Damn! Look, this is . . .

**Philip** *takes some heavy object, an award for industry statuette, and walks over to the gleaming high-tech Suck and Blow with its beautiful balloon gently breathing.*

Philip, no!!

**Philip** *smashes it, prompting dramatic flashes.*

Philip, that's our oxygen, you stupid little bugger!

**Philip**    It's still there, Chief, I've just knocked out the blower . . . Oh, I forgot to say, I also went back to the idea of killing myself . . .

**Chief** *moves to the desk, desperately punching buttons.*

Come on, Chief, you know the thing's on a timer. We're going to suffocate, so forget it. Let's think about something else . . .

**Chief**    You bloody lunatic!! (*He shouts.*) Help! Help! (*He turns back to* **Philip**.) What the hell's wrong with making a profit anyway . . . ?

**Philip**    Well, as I see it, there's profits and profits. (*He has to support himself, a bit gaspy.*) I mean, come *on*, Chief, surely you see, if you can't make a profit without selling your soul then you shouldn't be in business . . .

**Chief** (*staggering*)   Of course, you do realize you're sacked, don't you, completely and utterly sacked! You're sacked, your people are sacked, your people's people are sacked!! (*He falls over.*)

**Philip** (*on his knees*)   Decision received and respected, Sir . . . ! I think you should memo it, the screens won't lift for at least five minutes and we'll both be gone in half that time . . .

**Chief**   No, we bloody won't! (*He crawls to the windows, tries to force them.*)

**Philip** (*lying on his back*)   Senior waste of energy, Chief . . . Quite an interesting sensation really, this is how most people feel all the time . . .

**Chief** *moves to the desk.*

**Chief** (*gasping*)   I'm going to survive this, Philip, and so are you, and when we do, you're going to realize what a hugely detrimental career decision it is to try and kill your employer . . .

**Philip** (*lying on his back and gasping*)   It wasn't made lightly, Chief, believe me, I was so unsure I nearly rang my accountant.

**Chief**   Got it. (*He takes a gun from a drawer.*) We're going to make it, you little bastard, and when I've finished with you, you won't find a restaurant in WC1 that'll take your credit . . .

*He staggers to the windows and shoots at locks: 'Bang bang bang . . . click' And with a 'whhhirrrr', the screens rise up again, revealing the flickering orange and red of the flames. Again we hear the crump of explosions.*

**Philip** ( *fading*)    I'm drifting, Chief . . . I want you to know that although I have come to despise both myself and you as men . . . I think we bonded into a bloody senior corporate entity . . .

**Chief** *picks up the smashed Suck and Blow machine.*

**Chief** (*lurching towards the window with monumental effort*) I'll get some bloody air in here if it kills me . . . !!!

**Philip** (*nearly gone*)    Air, Chief?

**Chief** (*gasping*)    Just . . . smash the bloody window . . .

**Philip**    Can't help feeling you're forgetting something here . . .

**Chief** (*raising machine above his head with a huge effort*) We're going to live, Philip!!! And when we do, you bleeding heart liberal pansy, I'm going to kill you!

**Philip**    Chief, it's empty out there. There isn't anything left to bre . . .

**Chief** *hurls the machine through one of the windows.*

**Chief**    Done it!!

*A wind howls in, papers blow etc. The noise of explosions is suddenly huge.*

Done it, you bastard! (*He stands, taking a huge gulp. He turns downstage to face the prostrate* **Philip**. *A triumphant smile, which becomes glassy and transfixed as he can fool his lungs no longer and dies of suffocation.*)

*The fierce wind blows and the lights flicker.*

# Silly Cow

## Characters

**Sidney**
**Doris**
**Peggy**
**Douglas**
**Eduardo**

The action of the play takes place in the living-room of Doris Wallis's flat

**Time**: 1991

*Silly Cow* was first presented by Phil McIntyre by arrangement with Proscenium Productions Ltd at the Theatre Royal Haymarket, London, on 20th February 1991, with the following cast:

| | |
|---|---|
| **Sidney** | Patrick Barlow |
| **Doris** | Dawn French |
| **Peggy** | Victoria Carling |
| **Douglas** | Alan Haywood |
| **Eduardo** | Kevin Allen |

*Directed by* Ben Elton
*Designed by* Terry Parsons
*Produced by* Philip McIntyre

# Act One

## Scene One

**Doris Wallis**'s *flat. Morning.*

*There is a sideboard with drinks, glasses, two candelabras, and a bowl of fruit, including grapes. There is a TV set, a sofa, and a desk covered in papers and envelopes, and holding a typewriter a pen and a paper knife. On one of the walls, there is a mirror.*

**Sidney** *sits on the sofa. He likes to think of himself as a rough diamond. He is a populist tabloid newspaper man.*

**Sidney**   For Gawd's sake, Doris, pull your finger out; if you take much longer getting dressed you'll have gone out of fashion and have to start all over again.

**Doris** *emerges from her boudoir in her expensive, gaudy dressing-gown (kimono style), putting finishing touches to her hair. She is a big, bold, brassy, witty, women's features journalist; she has her own TV comment column which is pure abuse.*

**Doris**   Sidney, Sidney, Sidney, there may be cameras. You have to imagine what you're going to look like in the bitchy photo bit of some Sunday mag: 'Doris Wallis knew it would be curtains for her in court, so she decided to wear a pair . . .' The skirt might take a while, I'm afraid. Tight little black number, bought in a spirit of optimism, it's like trying to get a space-hopper into a gumboot.

**Doris** *retreats into her boudoir.*

**Sidney**   I must say this business of taking the press to court is becoming rather worrisome. Actresses, novelists, that murderer's missus. Where will it end? 'Is the press

to be shackled by an unhealthy obsession with the facts?'
we ask ourselves. It's going to make for some very dull
breakfast reading if everything we write has to be true.

**Doris** *emerges fully dressed.*

**Doris**    Well, what do you think?

**Sidney**    My darling, you look like mutton dressed as a
rat.

**Doris**    So you've been reading my new Fergie piece
then.

**Sidney**    Beautiful bit of work, like watching a
mugging. That's why you should be working for me.
The stuff is poetry, wasted on your current editor; the
clueless arse will probably print it upside down in the
sports page.

**Doris**    He won't be printing it at all at the moment; I
can't copy it through, my modem's down . . . This junk
was supposed to make our lives simpler! Let me tell you,
I've never had a postman go down on me.

**Sidney**    Well, quite. Tell you what, if you print it up,
I'll fax it through for you on the trusty portable.

**Doris**    Peggy does my admin, thank you, Sidney.

**Sidney**    Fair enough.

**Doris**    I shall put my trust in a simple envelope . . . A
couple of days won't matter either way, this piece is
timeless. 'Poor fatty Fergie looked like an explosion in
a pizza factory. Either the Duchess of Pork has gone
psychedelic or young Beatrice had just been sick.'

**Sidney**    Like I said, poetry. You really are a nasty
woman, my darling, creeping about making other
people's lives a misery. The world lost a great traffic
warden the day you opted for features journalism.

**Doris**    It's a dirty job but somebody has to do it. I'm the nasty cow who slaughters the sacred cows. Please feel free to have another bucket of Scotch. I'm going to finish my face.

**Doris** *exit.*

**Sidney**    Doris, darling. Believe it or not I do try and do a bit of work between drinks. Starting a new paper from scratch does require a modicum of time and commitment, especially if you've been away as long as I have. Nobody knows me in the UK any more and I have rather a lot to prove . . . So if you'll just sign this letter of intent then I can . . .

**Doris**    (*off*) Sidney, I haven't time . . . (*She snorts loudly.*)

**Sidney**    Call me old-fashioned, Doris, but I could have sworn you were supposed to put the powder on your nose not up it.

**Doris** *emerges perkily.*

**Doris**    Looking good is about feeling good, Sidney.

**Sidney**    Yes, well, I'd feel a great deal better with something a little more concrete to show my publishers. Bugger my boots, Doris, this is my break! English language editor of the first Euro tabloid! Think of it! Kelvin MacKenzie they could have asked, Derek Jameson, Larry Lamb, anyone, but no, they sent to America for little old nobody Sid!

**Doris**    Well, pardon me if I don't chew your trousers off right now and kiss the great man's bum.

**Sidney**    Doris!

**Doris**    I've said I'll probably take the job and I really don't see why I should have to sign anything.

**Sidney**   Three months I have courted you, my love, it's three long months since I wrote you from the States! I've got through entire marriages in less time than that.

**Doris**   I just have a problem with signing things, that's all. I think I must have been scared by a contract as a small child.

**Sidney**   Don't you trust me?

**Doris**   Of course I trust you, Candyfloss. I trust all editors to be dirty, duplicitous little weasels and not one has ever failed me.

**Sidney**   Doris, I have given up everything for this project.

**Doris**   You're not the only one who'll be giving things up, Sidney Skinner! You're not the only one who's had to work hard for everything they've got! While you were sneaking around Hollywood trying to buy photos of Jackie Onassis with her fun bags flying, I was dogsbody on the *Preston Clarion*, and I mean dogsbody.

**Sidney**   We all did our time in births and funerals, Doris.

**Doris**   Yes, and I'm never going back. These last few years I've finally got a grip of *la dolce vita* and I'm sticking my talons in deep. I am never again going to get up at five thirty on a rainy morning to report on a sheep-dog trial, I am never again going to cover the Liberal candidate in a by-election, and I am never again going to review another show at Preston Rep . . .

**Sidney**   Doris, this is all very interesting but . . .

**Doris**   There was this appalling old ham; I'd watched him every three weeks for two and a half years, and whatever part he played, he did his Noël Coward impression. Hamlet's ghost, Noël Coward. *The Crucible*,

Noël Coward; *Mother Courage*, Noël Coward. Imagine what the old fart was like when he actually had to play in a Noël Coward – his accent got so clipped I swear he was only using the first letter of each word. So please believe me, Sidney, I am never going back to that. I've done my time, Sidney, and now it's paying off. I've got my own column, I've cooked with Rusty on TV-AM, two *Blankety Blanks* last series, and Les called me Cuddles. What's more, tonight is the big one, I get my first *Wogan*. These are not things you throw away lightly, Sidney. Which is why I am just a little bit hesitant about ending up in Stuttgart working for an editor I scarcely know.

**Sidney**    Look, you're right to be cautious, Doris, but this is just a non-binding letter of intent to impress the krauts. I need something firm.

**Doris**    And as far as I'm concerned your krauts can shove something firm up their collective lederhosen. I don't like being pushed around and I certainly wouldn't dream of signing anything without showing it to Peggy.

**Sidney**    Gawd knows what you think you gain by showing it to Peggy anyway. You should be showing it to a lawyer.

**Doris**    If Peggy thinks it's necessary, she'll show it to a lawyer.

**Sidney**    She worries me that one. I can't say as I like her over much. She's a bit sly, two-faced.

**Doris**    Sidney, if Peggy had two faces I doubt she'd be wearing the sourpuss one she wears at the moment. Anyway I don't want you to like my staff. They're not there for you to like them. Now can you please shut up about Peggy, the letter, and the firmness of your krauts while I get ready for this bloody court case.

**Sidney**   Well, if you really want to know, I reckon that jacket's a bit much for Judge Jeffries.

**Doris**   Which just goes to show that you are a tasteless old tart and wouldn't recognize a good thing if it sat on your face and farted up your nose . . . These jugs are worth a character reference from the Archbishop of Canterbury. Not sexy, you see, jolly. Anyway it'll have to do, I'm not going to change again. Where the hell are my notes . . .

**Sidney**   Well, judging by the way you run your life, I presume Miss Piggy will have them.

**Doris**   I don't even know where the bloody court is. If she doesn't get here soon, knockers or no knockers, we shall lose this case by default . . .

**Sidney**   You rely on that girl far too much. She'll get poached by some Channel Four lefty who doesn't think it's a compromise to have a servant as long as he calls her a PA.

**Doris**   Lose Peggy? Don't, I wouldn't know where my arse was to wipe it.

**Sidney**   You're a sculptor, Doris, and the English language is your clay.

**Doris**   Thank you.

*We hear the sound of the front door slamming, a loud 'So-rry', and* **Peggy** *rushes in, briefcase and bag in hand. She has rather severe brunette hair and is efficiently, if slightly dowdily, dressed.*

**Peggy**   Sorry – that latch still isn't catching, you know, any manner of nasty type could just walk right in.

**Sidney**   I think one just did.

**Doris**   Peggy, where the hell have you been?! This is a bloody important day.

**Peggy**   Doris, I don't believe it. The car will be here in half an hour, Douglas is coming around to get the accounts signed, we still haven't got back to that *Wogan* researcher about tonight's show, and you haven't even changed.

**Sid** *laughs*.

**Doris**   Peggy, this is my court gear. Just because you choose to dress like you're applying for a mortgage. I am dressed to win. That bitch will take one look at these glad rags and confess to murdering Lord Lucan.

**Sidney**   Of course she will . . . Hallo Peggy.

**Peggy**   Good morning, Mr. Skinner.

**Doris**   Don't call him, 'Mister', Peggy, it gives him airs. The man doorsteps queer newsreaders for a living.

**Sidney**   We perform a valuable social service, my darling. After all, surely the public has a right to know which of its newsreaders are queer!

**Doris**   Well, of course it does, Sidney! The right to doorstep queer newsreaders is a cornerstone of our precious democracy! Take away that freedom and what have you got? *Pravda*, that's what!

**Sidney**   Well, quite. Anyway, Peggy, I've been oiling round your beautiful boss for three months now. I think you and I can insult each other on first name terms, eh? Go on, defrost that grimace, call me Sidney.

**Peggy**   Yes, but if the deal collapses and Doris decides she doesn't want to be your Euro features editor, that's when I think 'Mr Skinner' would be more businesslike.

**Sidney**   Well, you are certainly a cool one, aren't you?

**Doris**    Cool? Peggy can freeze a man at twenty paces; I swear sometimes when she opens her mouth a light comes on.

**Sidney**    Well, let me tell you, Doris, if you're thinking of letting her talk you into pulling this deal after I've spent three months with my tongue so far up your backside I know how many fillings you've got . . .

**Doris**    Oh, for pity's sake! Look, Peggy . . . Sidney wants me to sign this. He says it contains nothing binding.

**Sidney**    Of course it doesn't, it is simply a polite bloody note to a consortium of Huns who are considering paying you *mucho* marks and loadsa lira to say that you might be interested in becoming their resident Eurobitch. You are not committed, you are not bound, you will not wake up tomorrow to find *The Time Life History of the American Civil War* on your doorstep. All it does is give another little building block with which to assemble the deal.

**Doris**    Peggy?

**Peggy**    Mr Skinner's right, it's pretty innocuous, but I still wouldn't sign it, Doris. Why should you? If your present boss saw it . . .

**Sidney**    Present boss? What's your present boss got to do with anything? I was under the impression, Doris, that your present boss is about to become your ex-boss.

**Doris**    Oh, just give it here . . . Eyebrow pencil do?

**Sidney**    I think not. Blood would be acceptable.

**Doris**    Peggy, pen. There, satisfied?

**Sidney**    Satisfied? I don't think I'd go that far. Let us just say that for the time being I have returned the pills and the razor blade to the bathroom cupboard. (*He goes to the sideboard to pour himself a drink.*)

**Peggy**    Um, Mr Skinner, Doris and I have business to discuss and her car will be here at twelve to take her to court. I don't want to rush you . . .

**Sidney**    You won't, my darling, you won't. (*He pours himself a drink.*)

**Doris**    Twelve, Peggy! But we have to pick up Eduardo!

**Peggy**    Eduardo is being picked up first, he'll be in the car.

**Sidney**    Eduardo? Would that be the moody young fellow who was slouching on the sofa, grunting and absent-mindedly readjusting his wedding tackle last time I visited?

**Doris**    It would, and so what?

**Sidney**    I really don't think taking him to court is much of an idea, Doris. This toy boy thing of yours is rather naff. He can't be more than twelve.

**Doris**    Eduardo is twenty-one years old and we are very much an item. If he's on my arm coming out of discos but not beside me in my hour of travail, it's going to make me look a bit of a sad old bag, isn't it?

**Sidney**    If you think that the presence of a preening little juvenile delinquent with a courgette in his trousers is going to help your case, you don't know British justice.

**Doris**    Sweetheart, you have got your letter.

**Sidney**    Just finishing the old slurp.

**Doris**    Well, leave Eduardo out of this.

**Sidney**  All I'm saying is that, if you hear a gentle thud during the judge's summing-up, don't bother to look round – it will be Eduardo's balls dropping.

**Doris**  Sidney, do your Teutonic employers want a columnist, or do they want a celebrity columnist?

**Sidney**  Doris, fame is the spur.

**Doris**  Right, well, toy boys are the price you pay for a happening image like mine, so why don't you conserve your stupendous wit for the next waitress you are trying to impress, and let Peggy and me concentrate for one minute on this bloody case.

**Sidney**  Fair enough.

**Peggy** (*taking a newspaper cutting out of her briefcase*)  I phoned your brief again this morning and he says it could go either way. People are rather turning against the excesses of the press. Since the Cornwell business there's been Jeffrey Archer and Elton John and any number of . . .

**Doris**  Excesses! Give me that. (*She grabs the clipping, quoting.*) Look, here it is, Sidney: 'What, oh, what makes that silly cow Trudi Hobson think she can act?' and 'Was it a feminist statement to give the part to such a total dog?' . . .

**Sidney**  A robust but acceptable critique.

**Doris**  Good-natured, two-fisted, popular copy . . . (*She continues to read.*) 'Those huge, wobbling, quilted thighs, jammed up against the hem of her hot pants like two great, pink, floppy draught-excluders, made one pray for liposuction on the National Health . . .'

**Sidney**  Fair criticism.

**Doris**  Bold, brassy stuff. I just don't see the problem.

**Peggy**   I think she was hurt.

**Doris**   Hurt! My mother brought up five kids on a widow's pension.

**Peggy**   Now, that's not actually true, Doris.

**Doris**   Well, somebody's mother did. I cannot imagine what induced the silly cow to take offence!

**Peggy** (*taking the papers*)   As you well know, Doris, the centre of her case, apart from disputing the claim that she has concave breasts, and gargantuan love-handles, is the professional slur. You said she couldn't act. She's pushing the detrimental-to-her-employment thing hard, and six months out of work has added to her claim. You must take it seriously.

**Doris**   I love it when you're firm with me, Peggy. She's terribly pretty when she's firm, isn't she, Sidney?

**Peggy**   Doris, please. The case.

**Doris**   I said she couldn't act; Christ, if Roger Moore had been able to act, do you think he'd be the star he is today?

**Peggy**   Look, you really mustn't be flippant like this in court, Doris; the woman's a wreck, she's lost everything over this case. She was highly respected and you said . . . 'What with the disappearance of the rain forests, it was ecologically unsound of the Beeb to use such a wooden actress.'

**Doris**   But I say that sort of thing about everyone, I am the 'Ratbag of the Ratings'. Nothing is sacred – invalids, children; I once single-handedly destroyed a kid's career.

**Peggy**   Doris, it's not relevant . . .

**Doris**   Absolutely turned him into a national joke.
This repulsive, simpering little pre-pubescent tick,
looked like a bloody girl. Never stopped working,
Dickens' musicals, kids' adventures, became a sort of
national pet . . .

**Peggy**   Doris, we have to concentrate.

**Doris**   I thought, 'Right, my lad, I shall string you up
by your first pubic hair'. He did these ravioli ads,
grinning away saying, 'I wanta some more, Mama',
sucking up great mounds of the stuff, sounded like oral
sex in the elephant house. Every week for a month I
made a little joke about it. They ended up having to
ditch the campaign.

**Sidney**   God knows, Doris, I hope she doesn't win.
You've had poison in your pen for half a decade, you
could be going to court from now till Domesday. I saw
the clippings in America, they're dripping with blood.
That bit you did about the New, New Saint, I'm sure his
lunchbox would satisfy a starving mouse . . . and the
piece saying that bloke's Geordie accent, in the
Bleasdale, had arrived on Tyneside via Pakistan.

**Doris**   Look, I said she couldn't bloody act and she
had a couple of whopping great thunder thighs. I'm not
a serious critic, everybody knows that, I'm a bitch; my
TV page is a column, people read it for the bitching.

**Peggy**   The problem is, of course, the woman can
actually act a bit – Grotowski, Peter Brook, *Morecambe
and Wise Christmas Show*; a season at the RSC.

**Sidney**   Yes, she even came over and did her Juliet
and all that bollocks for us in the States.

**Peggy**   And you can be certain she'll bring that up
today.

**Doris**   Oh, and I suppose just because some bunch of over-subsidized, toffee-nosed, bulgie brains happen to appreciate her classical enunciation, our six and a half million readers have to grovel to superior beings, is that it?

**Peggy**   I think this is definitely one of your strongest cards. Our lawyer says the judge we've got will love the anti-intellectual bit; if she starts claiming a definitive Desdemona she's in trouble.

**Sidney**   The common touch, that's the way to play it.

**Doris**   Of course it is, people actually like my stuff, unlike the almighty RSC which people only pretend to like. We don't need a couple of million a year scrounged off the government to stay afloat.

*The door intercom buzzer sounds.*

Oh, God, that can't be Eduardo yet!

**Peggy**   I think it will be Douglas . . . (*She moves to the intercom.*)

**Sidney**   And who's Douglas, my dear? Surely not another pouting little three-year-old dago to lend emotional credibility to your case?

**Peggy** (*into the intercom*)   Hallo? . . . Mr Robertson. Please do come on up.

**Doris**   Douglas is my accountant, Sidney . . .

**Sidney**   Ah ha, an accountant, eh? A wolf in shit's clothing.

**Doris**   He's a decent bloke, Sidney. It'll be a new experience for you.

**Sidney**   And how would you know that he's a decent bloke? He didn't tell you so himself by any chance, did he?

**Peggy**    I told her so, Mr Skinner.

**Sidney**    Now, did you really, Peggy, so you're a financial expert as well as a legal one, are you?

**Peggy**    I took advice from Ms Wallis's bank manager, her agent, her solicitor and independent advisors . . .

**Sidney**    And no doubt came up with some Brylcreemed super yuppy with a portable phone strapped to his dick.

*There is a knock at the door.*

**Peggy**    Just push it, Douglas, the latch is faulty. (*She opens the door.*)

*Outside is* **Douglas Robertson**. *He is a dignified old gentleman, leather patches on sleeves, ancient leather briefcase. A kindly, but astute old fellow.*

**Doris**    Enter the yuppy.

**Peggy**    Hallo, Mr Robertson.

**Douglas**    Good morning, Peggy, my dear. How very lovely to see you.

**Doris**    Hallo, Douglas, it's a long way up, you must be knackered; come and sit down.

**Douglas**    It's thoughtful of you, Doris. Gravity does appear to exert something of a greater pressure on me than in years gone by.

**Peggy** *takes his coat.*

Thank you, Peggy. I'm sure that Newton missed a trick when he failed to equate increases in gravitational pull with advancing years.

**Doris**    He'd have spotted it quick enough if he'd been a woman, Douglas; I'll tell you, without a couple of RSJs

under these, (*She indicates her bust.*), I'd be polishing my
shoes with them.

**Sidney**    Nobody puts it like you put it, Doris.

**Douglas**    I don't believe I've had the pleasure, sir . . .

**Sidney**    Good thing too at your age. (*He laughs a
friendly laugh.*) Sidney Skinner, Doug, Doris's new boss.

**Doris**    Prospective boss, Sidney.

**Sidney**    Have it your own way, precious. Well, here's
to the lot of you. (*He drinks.*) Now, then, Doris, I know
your diary's about as crowded as the M25, so I'll just
take my letter and get out of your short and curlies . . .

**Peggy**    Um, Doris, I was wondering if, before Mr
Skinner goes, it might not be a good idea to let Mr
Robinson take a look at the letter you signed for him.
You know, just as a kind of . . . second opinion.

**Sidney** (*hating **Peggy***)    Darling, that is mine and
Doris's affair and none other's. Besides, as I keep telling
you, it's only a letter of intent. It is non-bloody-binding.

**Doris**    In which case, what's the problem?

**Sidney**    There isn't a problem! I just happen to
believe in the rights of privacy, that's all.

**Doris**    I shall remember that when you ask me to
stake out Elton John's bog.

**Doris** *exits to her boudoir.*

**Sidney** (*pompously*)    The lavatories of the famous are
news, Doris, it's completely different.

**Douglas**    Is this letter something you've signed,
Doris? You really must be most careful about things
which you are called on to sign.

**Sidney**  And what business is it of yours, mate?

**Douglas**  Excuse me, sir, but Doris's business is my business, I am her accountant.

**Sidney**  Exactly. A bloody ledger filer.

**Douglas**  It is an honourable profession.

**Sidney**  Honourable profession? What? Convincing the Revenue she spends a grand a week on pencils and Tippex. Listen, Doris, this letter has nothing to do with . . .

**Douglas** (*quietly very angry*)  Neither your letter nor your affairs interest me in the slightest, sir. I am here simply to complete Miss Wallis's accounts.

**Sidney** (*conciliatory*)  Well, of course you are. I didn't mean to be personal. I'll tell you what, if you're interested, I've just come back from donkey's years in the States and I've got a fairly substantial but rather dodgy pile hanging around off shore . . .

**Douglas**  It is quite clear to me the type of accountant that you favour, Mr Skinner. The type who supervised Doris's affairs until she came to me.

**Doris** *enters.*

**Doris**  Always have a straight accountant, Sidney. If you've got the dosh you can get away with most things in this country, but one thing Her Majesty won't stand for is not getting her cut. I can't think of anyone better placed to give us an honest opinion on your nasty little non-binding letter than Douglas . . . (*She grabs the envelope from Sidney.*) Would you mind, Douglas? (*She hands it to* **Douglas**.) Thank you.

**Sidney**  Yes, by all means take a look, Douglas, and then perhaps Peggy would like to have the bloody thing published in *The Times* so that everybody can get a sneak preview of our plans.

**Doris**    Oh, don't be such a drama queen, Sidney.

**Douglas**    Well, as Mr Skinner has so rightly pointed out, I am only an accountant, but even to my layman's eyes this document appears to be entirely innocent.

**Sidney**    Thank you.

**Douglas**    From the brief perusal I have made, it seems to be no more than a vague statement of possible future interest in a Pan-European publishing venture. (*He returns the envelope to* **Doris**'s *desk.*)

**Doris**    Thank you, Douglas. Better safe than sorry, Sidney.

**Sidney**    Well, you may rest assured that your new and loving boss will be going through your expenses with a nit comb once I've got you in my horrible clutches.

**Doris**    Goodbye, Sidney.

**Sidney**    Understood, a nod's as good as a wink. (*Draining his glass, he crosses to the table. To* **Peggy**.) And speaking of expenses, Peggy, let me assure you that personal assistants are not claimable. (*He snatches up the envelope from the crowded desk and makes for the door.*)

**Peggy**    Goodbye, Mr Skinner.

*The buzzer rings again.*

**Sidney**    Perhaps that's the milkman, perhaps Peggy would like me to show him the letter for a quick once over, just to be sure. After all, his brilliant milkman's eye may spot something sinister that a simple accountant might miss.

**Peggy** (*into the intercom*)    Hallo? What? But you're miles too early . . . oh, well, you'd better come up. (*She puts down the intercom.*) It's Eduardo.

**Sidney**   Oh, my Gawd, phone the society for the prevention of cruelty to children. Madam's jail-bait has arrived.

**Peggy**   I'm sorry about this, Doris, I distinctly told him twelve o'clock.

**Sidney**   He probably needs his nappy changing.

**Doris**   Sidney, hilarious though this paedo gag is, I consider it a touch rich coming from somebody who is going to be regularly exposing some poor sixteen-year-old bimbo's bazookas Europe-wide simply to provide Joe, Jacques and Juan public with the stimulus they require for their Euro stiffies.

**Sidney** (*pompously*)   The fun-loving photos in my newspapers will be there to express a joyful appreciation of the fulsome beauty of the youthful female form.

**Doris**   Sidney, they're there to help people wank.

**Douglas** (*very embarrassed*)   Uhm . . . perhaps I've called at an inconvenient time . . .

**Doris**   Well, you're here now, so don't worry about it.

*There is a knock at the door.* **Peggy** *opens it.*

**Eduaro** *stands outside. He is about twenty. A handsome, cocky, streetwise, male bimbo. He carries a bunch of flowers.*

**Eduardo** (*walking straight to* **Doris**)   He's here! Hallo, beautiful, what's shaking? Wicked little number, totally rockin'. I like a bit of purple. Wear it for me?

**Sidney**   Honestly, Doris, he'll have to go. See you.

**Sidney** *leaves.*

**Doris**    Eduardo, what the hell are you doing here . . .

**Peggy**    The car was supposed to pick you up at twelve.

**Eduardo**    Came early dinnit. Aren't you pleased to see me? Had me barnet done special. (*He checks his hair in the mirror, pleased.*) Murder or what? Raving, as it happens. Twenty-three notes, you can't knock it. Here's your good luck flowers . . . Hope you like them, you paid for them.

**Doris**    Peggy, do something creative with these, please.

**Peggy**    Of course. I'll put them in water, there's some in the lavatory.

**Douglas** *clears his throat.*

**Doris**    Oh yes, excuse me, Douglas, this is Eduardo, he's a friend of mine.

**Douglas**    Good morning, Eduardo.

**Eduardo**    Murder, Doug, happening. You one of Doris's toy boys then? Ha ha ha.

**Doris**    Douglas is my accountant, sweetie. Like you, he has to juggle with large and slightly unmanageable figures, but there the resemblance ends. Now then, sugar plum, Douglas and I have a bit of business to go over so you just sit tight and Peggy will make you a little drinkie.

**Eduardo**    Awesome. Er, tequila, Pegs. Actually I've got a bit of business for you myself, Doris.

**Peggy**    Tequila, Eduardo? You have to be in court in an hour.

**Eduardo**    Yeah, gonna be a banging good rave innit? Hope the judge has got a big wig, they're classic them wigs. Tasty or what? I went to court before, chillin' it was, we'd had E so we was wasted, but it wasn't really funny 'cos this Richard I knew got five years. Wish we could have stopped giggling 'cos he was a mate.

**Peggy**  Small tequila then? (*She goes up to fix a drink.*)

**Douglas**  Five years! Good lord, Eduardo, what had our friend done?

**Eduardo**  I told you. He was a Richard.

**Doris**  Peggy, Eduardo's drink quite quickly, please.

**Douglas**  But being called Richard isn't a crime.

**Eduardo**  No, the geezer dealt, Doug. He sold gear. Richard, Richard Gere, dealer, you thick or what? He sold . . .

**Doris** (*quickly*)  I agree with you Douglas, it does seem rather a harsh sentence for impersonating a film star.

**Eduardo**  Happening! Here, Dougy boy, have a look at this, eh? (*He crosses over and shows* **Douglas** *his wrist watch.*) Solid gold Rolex. Top watch. Murder innit? Two grand.

**Douglas**  It looks very . . . uhm . . . reliable.

**Eduardo**  I'll tell you what, mate, it's reliable bollocks, that's what, ha ha ha. Forty notes. Bangkok, totally rockin'. Have you ever been to Bangkok, Dougy boy? They've got chicks out there who can fire darts out their fou-fous . . .

**Doris**  Would you excuse me for a moment, Douglas?

**Douglas**  Of course, Doris. (*Rather embarrassed, he takes papers out of his briefcase and buries himself in his work.*)

**Doris** *beckons* **Eduardo** *over, tough and intimidating.*

**Doris**  Eddie?

**Eduardo**  What's shakin'?

**Doris**  Excuse me. (*She points at his mouth.*) This is your mouth. (*She points at his crotch.*) This is your brain. The distance between them is too far for a coherent thought to travel. So if you wish to continue drinking tequila and Hoovering up mirrors at my expense, you will not attempt to bridge the gap.

**Eduardo** (*slightly unconvincing bravado*)    Keep wishing, girl. You need me because I'm happening.

**Doris**  Eduardo, let me tell you an important fact of life. There are more penniless, loose little boys in the world than there are rich, single women. It's a buyers' market, sonny, and you're for sale. So back in your box.

**Eduardo** (*shaken but still attempting bravado*)    Oh yeah, I get you things you need . . .

*He produces an envelope and speaks the following to the room.*
**Peggy** *and* **Douglas** *are studiously ignoring them.*

Like, the newspaper clippings you asked for, you'll love them, they're fresh . . . (*Conspiratorially to* **Doris**.) Although some of the lines in them will get right up your nose, ha ha ha.

**Doris** *grabs the envelope.*

Now say you don't love me.

**Doris**  Eddie, this stuff is just like you. A cheap thrill, extremely common, and very easily purchased. Now then, Douglas, what can I do you for?

**Douglas**  Well, I'm rather worried about . . . (*He looks at* **Eduardo**.)

**Doris**  Oh, you can say your piece in front of

Eduardo, Douglas, he thinks a right-hand column is something to do with the way your trousers hang.

**Douglas**    Well, it's merely your VAT accounts, they have taken some considerable effort, for which, sadly, I shall have to invoice you, but I think I've got them straight. They merely require your signature and I shall be able to pop them in an envelope and send them to the Custom and Excise people . . .

**Doris**    Everybody wants my siggy today. Where do I sign?

**Douglas**    Well, I'd rather like to take you through them before you sign, Doris. One's financial affairs are not, after all, to be taken lightly.

**Eduardo**    Here, Peggy, did you know I can do a Kylie medley in burps?

**Doris**    Ed, mouth open, should be shut. Douglas, don't make me try to understand money, I love it too deeply, I love it with a passion, I want to sleep with it and have its babies. How can you ask me to see it as nothing more than columns, numbers and decimal points? Would you have asked Romeo to become Juliet's gynaecologist?

**Peggy**    Perhaps if you left them with us, Mr Robertson, Doris can go over them later and then I can get them biked round to you.

**Douglas**    Posting will be quite sufficient, Peggy. I confess this current vogue for entrusting one's every communication to some leather-clad Apache on a motorcycle leaves me rather cold. I would happily trade a day's delay in my affairs for the comforting sight of an English postman labouring up my path and laying his honest hand on my box.

**Doris**    Well, naturally.

**Douglas**    Since I know that you have a trying day ahead of you, Doris, I shall wish you the very best of luck in court.

**Doris**    Thank you and good luck with your postman.

**Douglas**    Thank you, Peggy . . . and um, goodbye, Eduardo.

**Eduardo** (*nearly ignoring him*)    Yeah, classic, Dougy, banging.

**Douglas** (*at a loss*)    Yes, well . . .

**Peggy** *moves to the door with* **Douglas**.

**Peggy** (*at the door*)    Thank you, Douglas, we'll be in touch.

**Douglas** *leaves*.

**Doris**    All right, Eduardo, go and wait in the car.

**Eduardo**    Haven't finished my drink.

**Doris** *crosses to him, grabs the drink*.

**Doris**    Bottoms up, my darling. You shouldn't drink so much anyway, it destroys the brain cells, which are not something you can afford to squander lightly. Now, go and wait in the car.

**Eduardo** (*sullenly*)    Yeah, well, I was going anyway, wasn't I. I'm just so wasted. Ravin' night last night.

*He slouches out.*

**Doris**    Sid's right, that one has to go.

**Peggy**    Where on earth did you get him?

**Doris**    Oh, he oiled his way up to me in some disco or other a couple of months ago. Luke-warm coffee, Pegs?

**Peggy** No thanks, Doris. I'll stick with my ginseng.

**Doris** Maniac. They all know good old Doris will buy them a few drinks and dust their nostrils. Don't know why I do it really; image, I suppose.

**Peggy** It isn't a particularly nice image, Doris.

**Doris** Yes, well, rather more acceptable than my real tastes, I think. The honest British housewife appreciates me standing up for womankind, but if she were to discover that I have been known to lie down with womankind, it would be something different altogether. Something, I fear, which would not go down too well with the ironing.

**Peggy** No, I suppose you're probably right.

**Doris** You see, it's different for gay girls. The media does at least have a place for camp, cosy, cuddly old puffs, in their fluffy jumpers. I'm not saying it's easy or pleasant, but there is a sort of niche. I think a cheeky lesbian would be rather more difficult to market, don't you? 'It's just after eight o'clock and time to go over to Doris the dyke with this morning's fashion tips' . . . It wouldn't work you see, the 'top knobs' would object.

**Peggy** I suppose they would.

**Doris** Of course they would. Men as a sex fancy themselves so much they just can't imagine anybody not fancying them.

**Peggy** But really, Doris, Eduardo? It's a pretty unpleasant cover story. I mean rather a high price to pay.

**Doris** Well, I don't sleep with him, do I? You silly cow. Anyway I like having bimbos to push around. People wouldn't think twice if I was a bloke and Eduardo was a dolly bird.

**Peggy**  I wasn't prying, Doris . . . I mean obviously I know what you . . . I mean, how you . . . well, the way you . . .

**Doris**  Of course you do, Peggy . . . (*Casually.*) After all, it takes one to know one, doesn't it?

**Peggy**  What?

**Doris**  Well, doesn't it?

**Peggy**  I . . . I don't know what you're talking about.

**Doris**  I think you . . . Anyway, better sign these accounts, get them out of the way.

**Peggy**  Aren't you going to check them?

**Doris**  What do you think I pay Douglas for? (*She takes up a pen.*)

**Peggy**  I'll read them through if you like . . .

**Doris** *signs the accounts.*

**Doris**  Too late. You may, at your leisure, bung them in an envelope and bike, post, or spiritually channel them back to dear old Douglas . . . Honestly, Peggy, what a morning! Sid gets worse, doesn't he? I mean, doesn't he? When God was making tosspots he certainly rolled his sleeves up for Sid.

**Peggy**  He does grate a bit I suppose.

**Doris**  I thank my lucky stars that the chances of me actually having to take his nasty little job in Stuttgart are pretty slim.

**Peggy**  I do have to say, Doris, that I can't quite see the need to be so enthusiastic with Sid. If you're really not thinking of taking his job why do you encourage him so much?

**Doris**   It's an insurance policy, Peggy, a second option. You never know, my telly plans might fall through, I certainly don't want to end up stuck in my present job.

**Peggy**   Oh, but they won't fall through, your ideas are wonderful . . .I finished typing up the treatment yesterday, I left it on the desk there in an envelope.

**Doris**   You may think my ideas are wonderful, Peggy. I certainly do, but unfortunately neither of us are commissioning editors at Channel Four and you just can't tell with Channel Four. They keep saying they want to go populist, but somehow they just can't resist those cartoons from Poland. That's why I'm stringing Sid along, just in case the telly falls through.

**Peggy**   Not really very ethical, Doris.

**Doris**   Please, Peggy, I'm going to cop enough character assassination in court.

**Peggy**   Yes, and speaking of which, you really must take it seriously, Doris. The thighs are definitely going to be a problem.

**Doris**   Why?

**Peggy**   Well the simple facts of the matter are that she couldn't (*She refers to the notes.*) 'tuck them into the top of her socks'.

**Doris**   But we went through all this with the lawyer. God knows how many months ago.

**Peggy**   Six and a half, I was still temping for the agency.

**Doris**   Don't know what I did without you, love . . . As I explained at the time, if these people set themselves up they should expect to be shot down. The bitch was asking for it.

**Peggy**    The question is, does accepting a role in a television drama series constitute asking to be called a silly, talentless, fat old cow.

**Doris**    As far as I'm concerned it does. Yes.

**Peggy**    I do wish I had your strength of purpose, Doris, I really do.

**Doris**    Well, I have a simple philosophy, Peggy, my love. When the dogs are eating the dogs, you have to make damn sure that you're the biggest bitch at the table.

**Peggy**    Well, it's all right for you, Doris, but some of us don't find it that easy. (*She bustles about getting* **Doris***'s stuff together.*) Is this your court bag, Doris?

**Doris**    Yes.

**Peggy**    I'm all right with accounts and business things, I can hide behind a schoolmistress pose and pretend to be tough dealing with old Sid, but real life's a bit more difficult to cope with. Just coming here today, for instance, there were three men hanging off the scaffolding. I mean it's not as if I'm exactly flaunting it is it? 'Beautiful arse, love, a smile wouldn't kill you though', two thoughtless seconds for those buggers and I spend the next two hours seething with fury.

**Doris**    I'll tell you what you have to do when that happens, Peggy. You must be nice and sweet, never sink to their level. You have to look up, give him a lovely smile, a little wiggle and then you say, (*With a big sweet smile.*) 'Fuck off and die, peanut prick'.

**Peggy**    God, you're a hard nut, Doris. I really do admire that.

**Doris**  I'm the hardest, Peggy. Bogeymen get scared at night imagining me under their beds. Listen, if people start bullying you, Peggy, you tell me, all right? (*She pats her hand and holds it.*)

**Peggy**  All right, Doris.

*Pause. There is a moment where more might be said between them. But the phone rings.* **Peggy** *answers it.*

Hallo, this is the personal assistant to Doris Wallis . . . yes, of course, a car at six, that's right . . . thank you, no, she will be made-up and wearing the clothes in which she intends to appear . . . Thank you, goodby . . . (*She puts the phone down.*) That was the *Wogan* people.

**Doris**  Oh God, *Wogan*!

*A distant car horn sounds.*

**Peggy** (*checking her watch*)  Eduardo's getting impatient. You're all right, Doris, it isn't quite twelve yet. Are you scared?

**Doris**  Scared, woman, don't be absurd. (*She puts on her coat.*) I shall return without a stain on my character or my underwear.

**Peggy**  Aren't you just a little bit sorry for this silly woman? I am a bit.

**Doris**  Good. Good, because it's when other people are feeling sorry that I'm at my happiest, Peggy. I have to be, I'm a journalist, I have to be pleased when other people are sad.

**Peggy** (*with a nervous laugh*)  You do enjoy cynicism, don't you, Doris?

**Doris**  I'm not being remotely cynical, I'm stating the obvious. I remember exactly the first time I realized the truth about my job . . . There was a bomb, you see, unexploded, and I knew I wanted it to go off.

**Peggy**    Oh, Doris, you didn't.

**Doris**    Of course I did. All of us poor runny-nosed hacks did. We'd stood waiting for hours. If it didn't go off, what would we have to show for a day's work? Nothing. Then it did go off and we were pleased.

**Peggy**    Yes, but you weren't actually pleased.

**Doris**    Peggy, I was delighted. It was a particularly good bomb too. It killed a little boy and a little girl . . .

**Peggy** (*upset*)    Doris, please, you don't mean that!

**Doris**    Peggy, if nobody dies, the article's on page six. I'm on page six. What do you want me to tell you? That I hope I never come across a decent story? That I hope I never get a page one byline?

**Peggy**    Well, no, news is news, it isn't wrong to want to report it . . .

**Doris**    And what happens when you stop reporting news and start looking for it? For instance, you've got your sports hero, the new footballer; my editor wants some news: 'Does he screw around? Does he beat his wife?' . . . So I dig and I dig and it turns out the man is a decent bloke. What's my reaction? It's the same as the bomb, Peggy, I'm angry, I'm frustrated, I swear I am sat at my desk wishing that a man beat his wife!! That isn't very nice, is it, Peggy?

**Peggy**    Well, no but . . .

**Doris**    No, it isn't. I know how tough I have to be to do my job. I know I certainly do not require hysterical self-indulgent actresses getting a judge to run it in. (*She puts on a scarf.*) I'll see you when I see you.

**Peggy** (*emotionally*)    Good luck, Doris. I'll be with you all the way.

*The lights fade down.*


## Scene Two

*After a couple of seconds the lights come up. It is late afternoon.*

**Doris** *puts her bag back down again and takes off her coat. She has returned from court elated.*

**Doris**    The prisoner has returned!!

**Peggy**    Doris!

**Doris**    Champagne, Peggy, bugger *Wogan*, I'll do it a bit sloshed. I want to get so full of fizz, if I uncross my legs I'll shoot out of the window.

**Peggy** (*anxiously*)    So you pulled it off? You got away with it?

**Doris**    'Pulled it off! Got away with it!!' I wasn't flogging a dodgy car, woman! I was defending my honour and professional integrity. I didn't 'get away' with anything. I wittily, elegantly, and with great restraint shat on her and rubbed her face in it.

**Peggy**    So I take it you won, then?

**Doris**    Not quite actually won, no, but as good as. They upheld her claim, but get this, Judgie said he was sick of these big libel awards and that, personally, he thought that saying a girl had gargantuan love-handles was a compliment and advised the jury accordingly. She got a tenner damages and no costs.

**Peggy**    No costs! She'll be completely bankrupt, ruined.

**Doris** (*mock seriously*)    I know, Peggy, and I'm devastated, perhaps you'd better phone the Samaritans before it all becomes too much for me.

**Peggy** *gets the champagne.*

**Peggy**    All right, all right, I was only remarking.

**Doris**    A symptom of your celebrated weakness, Peggy, you must toughen up.

**Peggy**    All right, tell me every little mouth-watering detail.

**Doris**    Mouth-watering is exactly the word, Peggy, this case was the legal equivalent of an Opal Fruit. Wait for it, you are simply not going to believe this. They actually measured the silly cow's saddle bags in court.

**Peggy**    No!

**Doris**    Some old bailiff, you know the type, face like a gas bill, had to scurry off for a tape measure . . . He came back all solemn with a little bag from Woolworth's, 'Ninety-two centimetres in trousers, m'lord', he says . . . I have never seen a woman look a more complete turd in my entire life. I'll tell you what, she's earned her tenner.

**Peggy**    It must have been excrutiating.

**Doris**    We cringed . . . All except the judge, that is, he's getting all frisky and chipping in that either way a fellow likes something to grab hold of. It was comedy mayhem, believe me.

**Peggy**    Ninety-two centimetres had better not be big; I must be about that or more . . .

**Doris**    Of course it isn't big, which I suppose is one of the reasons why the silly cow won her case. But the reason she's got nothing out of it is because she's a stupid self-righteous shit and we could all see it. I said it, I said to the judge, I said, 'Come off it, Judgie!'

**Peggy**  You didn't!

**Doris**  Well, something like that. I said, 'It's bloody obvious that Trudi Hobson is a beautiful woman; she is pert, gorgeous and chewable, with ravishing blonde hair and a lovely figure . . .' I said, 'If a woman like that can't take a good-natured slagging, Gawd help us poor dogs who live in the real world. There are people out there dying of cancer, for God's sake!'

**Peggy**  You don't live in the real world, Doris . . .

**Doris**  (*enjoying her champagne, draining the glass and refilling it*)  Minor point. People think I do. Anyway the judge was lapping it up, wasn't he? Not often for him he gets a dock full of sauce buckets debating the size of their fondle fins. Lucky for me he was a jolly old goat, he was leering away from the start with his wet, watery, yellow eyes, shining like a couple of raw eggs.

**Peggy**  Was she playing up to him?

**Doris**  Was she hell. She was glaring at the floor, I've seen more moving performances in a Renault ad; but I was giving it full cleavage, nothing too obvious, you know, (*She thrusts our her chest.*) just that look I've got that says 'wrap these round your ears, mate, and I'll breathe on your bald patch'.

**Peggy**  Didn't the prosecution say anything?

**Doris**  What could they say? 'Objection, m'lud, but will you kindly stop leering at the defendant's coconuts.' There are certain things you just don't tell a judge, Peggy. Anyway, then we got into the bit about acting. God you would have loved it . . . She said she had brought the case on behalf of all those in the public eye who were at the mercy of a new breed of gutter journalism.

**Peggy**    Sounds a bit righteous.

**Doris**    Made me want to carpet the court. I said, 'Judgie, this is nothing more than special pleading from a typically self-obsessed actress. So I said she couldn't do her job? There are kids out there taking heroin and nobody gives a damn!!'

**Peggy**    And was this argument judged admissable?

**Doris**    Well, not really, the judge told me to stick to the point but he was nice about it. Luckily for me this woman was her own worst enemy. She called me a brute and a bully. Can you believe it, a bully! It was like something out of a *Girl's Own* annual. A bully. I just said I was entitled to my opinion and that she simply could not act. I was sorry but she was a wooden, lifeless performer with all the genuine histrionic talent of a weatherman and it was my duty to express that fact to the public.

**Peggy**    And what did she say?

**Doris**    She cried, the bitch. I could see the judge going gooey, so I said that crying, m'Lord, is one of the best performances she would ever give; the court loved it.

**Peggy**    Did anyone mention the RSC?

**Doris**    Of course they did, and that was when I clinched it. I mean honestly, Peggy, apart, of course, from the RSC, who gives a toss about the RSC? Ninety per cent of the population never visit the theatre. Nine per cent of the remaining ten have a nice Aberdeen Angus and then go and see *The Milkman's Got My Trousers*, and who goes to the RSC? Eight rows of

ponces on the mailing list and fifteen hundred extremely
pissed-off school kids.

**Peggy**    I don't know if that argument's really fair,
Doris.

**Doris**    Of course it's fair. Anyway, the court must
have thought it was fair because, as I say, she won
technically but lost in reality, and I, my faithful friend,
am off the hook.

**Peggy**    Well, congratulations, Doris, thank God it's
over.

**Doris**    Over for me, I don't think it will ever be over
for her. I truly believe she's gone completely mad. After
we left the courtroom she sort of flipped. She ran up to
me and, quite frankly, I've never seen such hatred in
anyone. She started to scream at me.

**Peggy**    What did she say?

**Doris**    She said . . . Oh, it's too bloody stupid, let's
forget it.

*Evening is falling, the curtains are still open, and very slowly, it is
getting darker.*

**Peggy**    What did she say, Doris?

**Doris** (*quietly*)    She said I was going to die.

**Peggy** (*concerned*)    Not really?

**Doris**    Yes, really. Die publicly. Scorned and
humiliated just as she had done.

**Peggy**    I knew this woman wouldn't be stopped by a
judge. She needs help.

**Doris** (*suddenly screaming*)    'Viper! Slut! Filthy
cockroach!!!'

**Peggy** (*shocked*)   Please, Doris.

**Doris**   That's what she called me. Right outside the courtroom. Her make-up was all tear-streaked and caked, and she was wearing plenty of it. I have never seen a woman with so much make-up on; she looked like a witch with psoriasis. She threw herself down in front of me and started to tear at her clothes.

**Peggy**   What? In front of everyone?

**Peggy** *has hardly finished her question when* **Doris** *hurls herself down before her, grabbing at her.*

**Doris** (*screaming again*)   'Yes, yes, you're going to die! I swear I'll make you die. You have no human heart, you cannot feel, your soul is the soul of a witch. It is rotten, cold and dead and you must die! You're poison, do you hear me?! Bitter, bitter gall!' And then she turned and ran for a taxi, as if the hounds of hell were after her.

**Peggy**   Poor woman.

**Doris**   Yes, I must confess I felt a twinge. (*After a slightly thoughtful pause, snapping out of it.*) Still, sod her, eh? We won! (*She drains her glass.*) And tonight we celebrate.

*Black-out.*

# Act Two

*The same. Immediately following.*

*The lights come up to find* **Doris** *raising her empty glass.*

**Doris**   Champagne and pizza, that's what we need!
Plenty of time before the Wogan car comes.
Champagne and pizza is the food of the gods and I'm
going to stuff it, I'm going to shove it, I'm going to
smear pizza all over my body, till I can do an impression
of a car crash . . . (*She grabs the phone and dials.*) What do
you want on yours, Pegs? I'm having the lot . . .

**Peggy**   Oh, just a vegetarian please, no peppers, no
chilli, no capsicum.

**Doris**   A vegetarian, no peppers, no chilli, no
capsicum . . . ! (*Into the phone.*) Hallo? Look, I'm afraid I'm
going to have to call you back. I appear to be ordering
for Mahatma Gandhi. (*She puts the phone down.*) Peggy,
this is a celebration, you cannot order a dry pizza base.

**Peggy**   I'm not, I want cheese and tomato, it's called a
Neapolitan.

**Doris**   A pizza, Peggy, by any other name would be as
crap. Calling it a 'Neapolitan' means nothing, you could
call Little and Large the 'Neapolitan' Brothers and
they'd still be two Mogadons in velvet bow-ties. This is a
party and Neapolitans are not invited.

**Peggy**   All right, I'll have a few mushrooms.

**Doris**   Then let the orgy begin. (*She dials again.*) This is
the start of a whole new time for me, Peggy, I can feel it.
I've dealt with that jumped-up actress, I've got more
career options than an ex-cabinet minister, I'm about to

order a pizza! I'm in Heaven.

**Peggy**    Beware hubris, Doris.

**Doris**    What's that, something peppery? All right, I'll
tell them to hold the hubris.

**Peggy**    It's Greek.

**Doris**    Oh, I love all that stuff, chick-pea, fish roe . . .

**Peggy**    It's an ancient Greek term. It means pride
comes before a fall.

**Doris**    Well, who's a Mrs Hoity Toity . . . (*Into the
phone.*) No, not you, I've just got a classically educated
killjoy ordering at this end. All right, got your pen
ready? I'd like one (*Jokingly scornfully.*) 'Neapolitan',
please, with three and a half mushrooms, and two, very
large, very deep whoppers, with everything on, yes,
that's right everything you've got, the tables, the chairs,
the phones, extra hubris. If there is a restaurant cat,
slaughter it, put the meat on one and the pelt on the
other. Cheesecake, fudge cake, and garlic bread twice.
Good, that's the penthouse flat, Morley Mansions. And
could you send a slightly less hormonally imbalanced
adolescent this time. The last lad who came, I nearly
tipped the pizza and ate his face . . . Ta, gorgeous. (*She
puts the phone down.*) Now then, Peggy, let's have another
glass of that fizz. I feel fantastic.

**Peggy**    It really is good to see you so happy, Doris.
You didn't say anything but I knew you were worried
about that case.

**Doris**    Well, the woman was so determined, I thought
she might sway the judge by just being a mad old witch.
That scene outside the court proves she's a lunatic. Yes,
there's no question, I'm glad it's over and I can
concentrate on the future.

**Peggy** *brings more champagne.*

**Peggy**    Yes, let's drink to the future.

**Doris**    Up yours, Peggy. It looks pretty bright to me. I'm on a roll, Peggy, everything is opening up for me, and what's more I want you to be a part of it.

**Peggy**    Well, I want to be a part of it, Doris, you know that, but it's not easy.

**Doris**    Now don't be stupid. We've become a team, you and I. Whether I stay in London or go to Stuttgart, you've got to be there.

**Peggy**    Oh, you won't be going to Stuttgart, silly, you know Sid's horrible job is a last option. You'll get the telly.

**Doris**    Well, stranger things have happened.

**Peggy**    I must say I'm a bit concerned about that letter he made you sign though. Supposing you let Sid down and then lost the telly, you'd have to stay where you are. That letter would be a nasty little document to end up on your current editor's desk.

**Doris** (*happily slightly tiddly*)    Peggy, please, I want you to imagine that this small bunch of grapes is our friend Sidney's testicles. (*She snips off the grapes.*) Now, were that man to do the dirty on me, I swear, Peggy, I should have his scrotum (*She drops the grapes into the machine.*) wrapped round my carriage return and . . . (*She types the keys very hard.*) write his epitaph on them! (*She finishes and viciously slams the carriage return.*)

**Peggy** (*reprovingly*)    Well, you're planning to do the dirty on him, Doris.

**Doris**    I am an artist, Peggy, can I help it if I'm being extensively courted?

**Peggy**   You're being extensively deceitful.

**Doris**   That's my prerogative, I'm the one with the talent, let me tell you, Pegs! Once I get a proper shot at telly, all the European Currency Units in Germany wouldn't get me back to print.

**Peggy**   I'm sure they'll take your idea, it's so wonderful, so many shows in one – a talent show, a magazine, a chat show, a weekly review. The title's brilliant.

**Doris** (*standing exuberantly with her glass*)   *A View from the Bitch.*

**Peggy**   I did laugh while I was typing it, when I wasn't trying to decipher your shorthand. Did you really mean *Eurovision Pong Contest*?

**Doris**   I most certainly did. It's a Demean the Public section. Guess a bloke's nationality by smelling his breath.

**Peggy**   Oh, I see.

**Doris** (*rummaging on the table*)   So where is this bloody treatment then? I want to make sure you got the Mugging section right.

**Peggy**   Well, it made sense to me. Basically it seems to be a question of taking a handbag from a woman in the audience and showing everybody else what's in it.

**Doris**   You'll never be a poet, Peggy . . . Oh, look, can you believe it? (*She finds an envelope.*) Sidney didn't take his letter after all, drunken old fool.

**Peggy**   I'm sure he did, I saw him take it.

**Doris**   Well he must have put it back, honeyplum, because it's still here and so we remain gloriously uncommitted.

**Peggy** (*concerned, looking over the table*)    Doris, the treatment I typed for you was in an envelope like that . . .

**Doris** (*worried*)    What? You mean it looked like this? (*She holds up* **Sidney**'s *letter.*)

**Peggy**    I . . . I think so . . . (*She realizes.*) Oh, my God.

**Doris**    So we've got Sid's letter and he's got my treatment. (*Urgently.*) Get Sid on the phone . . .

**Peggy** *is halfway to the phone when the door intercom buzzer sounds.* **Peggy** *and* **Doris** *look at each other.*

It can't be the pizzas, it'll take a month to cook what I ordered . . .

**Peggy** *crosses to the intercom and answers.*

**Peggy**    Hallo? . . . Oh, hallo, Mr Skinner . . . Yes, come on up.

**Doris**    Shit.

**Peggy**    He sounded all right.

**Doris**    If he's taken a look in that envelope there's no way he's going to be all right.

**Peggy**    What if he just sent it straight off? I mean, what will the Germans make of it?

**Doris**    Oh, we'll get away with that, I can't see them making much out of the Eurovision Pong Contest. But if he's read it . . . Oh, well, we shall see, Peggy.

*A knock at the door.* **Peggy** *opens it.*

**Sidney** *is outside.*

**Sidney** (*cheerfully*)    Hallo, Peggy.

**Peggy**    Hallo, Mr Skinner.

**Sidney**    Doris, darling, you won't believe it but your old pal must have had a brain transplant with a house brick. After all that bloody fuss over the letter . . .

**Doris**    I know, you forgot it. (*She has it in her hand.*)

**Sidney**    Gawd, am I thicker than an elephant's sandwich or what? (*He takes it from her.*) Thank my stars, thought I might have lost it. (*He takes the paper up stage and, with his back to the audience, puts his briefcase on the sideboard. He opens the case as if to put the paper in; there seems to be a bit of fussing around. Cheerily.*) Well now, Doris, you old jailbird you, tell old Sidney how you got on in court today. I didn't see anything on the news.

**Doris** (*still not knowing how to play it*)    Rather well, actually. I won, basically. Although the silly cow went completely mad afterwards and threatened me with death outside the court.

**Sidney**    Blimey, that's a bit upsetting, I must say.

**Doris**    Oh, don't worry about it, she's harmless enough. All actresses are completely bonkers, they have lobotomies and electric baths at drama school. Ha ha ha!

**Sidney**    No, I mean it's a shame about you winning your case. I don't deny that seeing you dragged off to Holloway in chains would give me greater satisfaction than touching up the gusset on a blurred telephoto shot of Princess Stephanie's crotch.

**Doris**    I beg your pardon.

**Sidney**    You, Doris, are a lying, two-faced slag.

**Doris**    So you read the treatment then?

**Sidney**    Yes, I read it. Congratulations, it was very, very good. Rather a complex show to pull off whilst holding a full-time job in Stuttgart, of course, but nonetheless, very, very good.

**Doris**   Thank you.

*An embarrassed pause.*

**Peggy** (*nervously*)   Um, drink, Mr Skinner?

**Sidney** (*without looking at her*)   Fuck off, Peggy.

**Doris**   Um, I'd rather you didn't address my friends like that.

**Sidney**   Oh, friend, is it? I thought she was just some downtrodden little wage slave . . . (*To* **Peggy**.) I hope you realize, Peggy, that you're probably next under Doris's dancing duvet. Has she started suggesting you wear something prettier yet? Something pink and lacy. Take care, my little virgin prune, this nasty old slut will be under your hem like a greased whippet.

**Doris** (*suppressing great anger*)   And just what is all that supposed to mean, Sidney?

**Sidney**   Come off it, darling one. It's a bit stomach-turning watching a wicked old devil like you trying to play the innocent. Everybody knows about your little preferences, don't they? Except that sad bit of juvenile rough trade, Eduardo, you drag around . . . He knows now though, I rung him. Cor, those Latin types can't half swear.

**Doris**   Bit pathetic, wasn't it, Sidney? Telling tales to some dirty, stoned kid . . .

**Sidney**   I'm going to make you regret your lack of standards, Doris.

**Doris**   Oh, for God's sake, all right, I've been investigating other work. So what? It probably won't come off, and then you and I will be spitting blood at each other in Stuttgart as if nothing had happened.

**Sidney**    I'm not going to Stuttgart. I've already faxed them, I've blown it out.

**Doris**    Sidney, you're raving. You reckon that because I've been a bit of a naughty girl, you're going to make yourself redundant?

**Sidney**    I'm not going to be redundant, darling. At least I hope not. If negotiations that I put in train this afternoon come off, I'm going to be fronting an outrageous new talent, magazine, chat show on Sky TV.

**Doris** (*very heavily*)    What are you talking about, Sidney?

**Sidney**    Oh, I know it seems unlikely, dear. An old tart like me becoming a star, but I have got a certain common touch, don't you think? And anyway, the ideas I had to offer, well, the producer had a bloody orgasm. I must say, I thought he'd be pleased, ideas were rather good you see . . . the 'Pong' contest, the handbag bit, great for a man to do it too.

**Doris** *starts forward.* **Sidney** *grabs a bottle.*

Don't you bloody hit me, you gorilla-faced dyke!

**Doris**    I'll sue you for plagiarism . . . !!

**Sidney**    Oh, yeah? Who have you got? You and your mousy little girlfriend here? Don't make me damp my jocks. I'll get a witness too, I'll get ten. Copyright is about proving first ownership, my gorgeous old sauce. My idea's with a producer at Sky, who's seen yours?

**Doris**    Sid, you pig, if you pull this off, which you won't let me tell you, I shall crucify you every week in

print for ever. What I did to that silly cow in court today
will look like a character reference from Postman Pat.

**Sidney**    Not in your present rag it won't, my dear.
You see, as I believe I mentioned earlier, this case has a
portable fax machine in it, Cellnet you see, very clever.
(*He takes the letter of intent out again.*) I didn't think that your
current editor would take kindly to you signing a letter
of intent to German publishers, so I've sent him a copy.

**Doris**    You . . . didn't!

**Sidney**    I did, my love. Faxed it through to him just
now. If the lazy sod's still at work, he'll have it by
now . . . (*He walks to the door.*) So there you go, Doris,
Europe's out, you've almost certainly lost your present
job, and I've nicked your game show. That is what you
get for being a dirty double-crosser.

**Sid** *exits.*

**Doris** *rushes to the door and shouts after him.*

**Doris**    You're dead, do you hear me, Sid, dead!

**Peggy**    I'm so sorry, Doris . . .

**Doris**    I can't believe it, the bastard, I've got to
think . . . Why did you make me drink that bloody
champagne, Peggy? I've got to think . . . I need
something to help me think . . . (*She crosses to the sideboard.
She is looking for something. She searches for a moment.*) Peggy,
I've told you never to clear anything up, or throw
anything away from here.

**Peggy**    I haven't . . . What . . .?

**Doris**    An envelope that Eduardo brought round . . .
There was an envelope here when I left for court!!

**Peggy**    An empty envelope, yes . . .

**Doris**   It wasn't bloody empty! It had a little package in the bottom of it, an important little package.

**Peggy**   A package of what?

**Doris**   Never mind what, where's the bloody envelope?

**Peggy**   I . . . I . . . used it.

**Doris**   Peggy, what do you mean?

**Peggy**   I always re-use old envelopes . . . I've got these re-sealing stickers from Friends of the Earth . . . It was empty, I . . .

**Doris** (*shouting*)   It wasn't bloody empty!!

**Peggy** (*very upset*)   Please Doris, don't shout, I don't understand. What was in it?

**Doris**   Never mind what was in it, who did you send it to?

**Peggy**   It was your VAT tax forms from Douglas.

**Doris** (*exploding in disbelief*)   The Customs and Excise!! You sent eight grams of cocaine to Her Majesty's Customs and Excise!!

**Peggy**   Cocaine? Doris, I had no idea you . . .

**Doris**   Where's my passport? I've got to pack! Peggy, phone the travel agent, I have to get out. Oh, my God! I've got to pack! This can't be happening!

**Peggy**   I didn't send it to Customs, I sent it to Douglas.

**Doris**   Douglas?

**Peggy**   That was what I was supposed to do, wasn't it?

**Doris** (*stopping*)   Douglas? That's better . . . probably wouldn't even know what it was, don't think he'd shop me . . . Peggy, get him on the phone . . .

**Peggy** *grabs the phone.*

Look at these, Peggy . . . (*She goes to her desk, starts grabbing handfuls of envelopes.*) Envelopes, envelopes, we are surrounded by hundreds of bloody envelopes . . . Peggy, the trees are already dead, I don't think they would have minded . . . Oh, God, why me!

**Sidney** *appears at the door again, with* **Eduardo**.

**Sidney**   Knock, knock. Excuse I. Just wait and see who I've found, trying to kick the door down; he's bust your outside lock . . . Thought I'd bring him up, wouldn't want to miss the fun.

*He leans arrogantly against the door as* **Eduardo** *pushes past him.*

**Peggy** (*to* **Doris**)   Douglas is out. (*She puts the phone down, crosses to the door.*) Eduardo, this isn't a good time.

**Eduardo** *is furious – seething with injured pride. He looks ready for violence.*

**Eduardo**   Oh, yeah, Pegs doll? I reckon it's a raving good time. Awesome. Anybody want a couple of lines of Gonzales? It's top gear, banging good stuff. 'Columbian'. Got it off a Rasta. Totally wasted my box. Murder, man.

**Doris**   Get out, Eduardo. I'll phone you.

**Eduardo**   You can stick your phone up your brown-eyed cyclops, you horrible old tart.

**Doris**   What?

**Eduardo** (*shouting*)   Why didn't you tell me you was a muff muncher?

**Doris**   Listen, sonny, I'll tell you exactly what I like and when I like, and what I'm telling you now is to fuck off and take your foul, fucking mouth with you.

**Eduardo** (*beginning to let his anger show*)   Listen, babes, I don't mind being pampered but I ain't being used, all right? I got standards. I'll take 'em fat, I'll take 'em ugly, but I don't take them queer. You made a fool of me. You . . . you made me look dirty in front of the geezers.

**Doris**   Excuse me, but this is now becoming just a touch comical. I've had a tabloid editor talking about privacy, now I've got a rather inexpensive toy boy saying he feels soiled. Well, you are soiled, Eduardo, that's how you were born. Brillo pads and Liquid Gumption couldn't raise the ghost of a shine on you.

**Eduardo** *leaps forward and grabs her.*

**Eduardo**   Yeah, and you're a dirty pervert! Your sort should get put away! Bloody corrupt kids you do!

**Peggy**   You leave her alone you . . . peanut prick!

**Eduardo** *turns on* **Peggy**.

**Eduardo**   What's shakin' now, eh? What's cooking, Pegs? Raving got you, ain't I? Raving got you, you old dog. (*He raises his fist to strike.*)

**Peggy**   Hit a woman would you, you coward!

**Eduardo**   Why not? I ain't Saint raving George, am I? Besides, your kind ain't women. Bet you molest kids, it's always in the papers that stuff is. Makes me want to have a right classic spew.

**Doris**   Peggy, phone the police, tell them we have two dangerous intruders . . .

**Eduardo** *calms quickly.*

**Eduardo**   No need for all that.

**Sidney**   Oh, don't trouble yourself on my behalf, I shall be off shortly. Just finishing my drink and watching the fun . . .

**Doris**   All right, Peggy.

**Eduardo** (*triumphantly*)   You want to know something, Doris! You thought you kept your little secret pretty good, didn't yah? Well, I've blown it, yeah, classic giggle. Stitched you up proper, you slag. Want to know what I did? I told the papers. Awesome, eh? I told them about us and what you really are . . .

**Sidney**   'Teenage toy boy denounces middle-aged celebrity girlfriend as gay.'

**Doris**   I am not middle-aged!

**Eduardo** *goes to the door.*

**Eduardo**   So see you, doll, gonna have a decent rage for once, ain't I? Do some blow, get on some 'E'. Hang out with some happening people, people who ain't half dead. You won't see me again. Except one thing, babe, we'll be together one more time, in the Sunday papers, ha ha ha! Awesome, eh?

**Sidney**   Thank you for the drink, Doris . . . Actually, you won't believe this, but I'm sorry. You're having a slightly more rotten evening than even I had planned.

**Doris**   You've got five seconds.

**Sidney**   OK. Just trying to be nice.

**Sidney** *pauses for a second, then exits.*

*Long pause.*

**Peggy** (*pretty shaken*)   What . . . what are we going to do, Doris?

**Doris**   Something very strange is going on, Peggy, too much is happening at once.

**Douglas** *appears at the door. He is stern and angry. He is holding the envelope.*

**Douglas**   The outside door lock has been forced, I presume by those two hooligans I just passed on the stairs. Anyway, I took the liberty of coming up.

**Peggy** *and* **Doris** *jump.*

**Doris**   Hallo, Douglas.

**Douglas** (*sternly*)   Good evening, Miss Wallis.

**Doris** (*nervously correcting him*)   Doris, Douglas.

**Douglas**   I think under the circumstances I would prefer a less familiar form of greeting.

**Doris**   Circumstances, Douglas?

**Douglas**   I was with the Customs and Excise for fifteen years, I know the hellish stuff when I see it.

**Doris**   Well, don't cry about it, for God's sake. It's only for private, recreational . . .

**Douglas**   Oh, private is it? Damn strange kind of privacy, popping it in with your VAT returns and sending it to your accountant. It's the breathless arrogance of your kind that makes me so very angry. Why do you consider yourself so different, Miss Wallis? Why is it that people like you, fashionable people, can indulge yourselves in any kind of unhealthy, antisocial activity that you choose and continue to lead comfortable, respectable lives while half the civilized world watches its children die over stuff like this . . . (*He shakes the envelope at her.*)

**Doris**   Look, Douglas I'm having a particularly tough day today and I'm not sure I'm up to a moral debate.

**Douglas**   No! No, I don't think you are up to a moral debate, you nasty, hypocritical woman.

**Doris**   Douglas, I'm sorry the stuff has offended you so much, I really am, and I'll think about what you've said . . . but, for now, why don't you give it me back and then you can forget all about it, eh?

**Douglas** (*very angry*)   Do you know there are Asian women doing fifteen years in Holloway for getting this stuff to you? Poor, clueless mules. I know, I caught a few, and a bloody depressing business it was too. Fishing small, damp packages out of people's bottoms made me feel like a bloody magician.

**Doris**   Yes, well, I'm very sorry for them . . .

**Douglas**   Good! Good! I'm glad you're sorry for them, it's nice that you're sorry for them, because you're shortly going to have the pleasure of being able to tell them so yourself.

**Peggy** (*stunned*)   Douglas, no!

**Doris**   What the hell are you talking about, Douglas?

**Douglas**   Oh, come now, Miss Wallis, you know me well enough to realize that I am not and never have been one of these types, so common in the last decade, who believe that they need only obey those parts of the law which they choose. Oh, well, I know you think me a senile old fool.

**Doris**   Yes.

**Douglas**   It doesn't matter anyway, I just wanted you to understand my point of view. It's a police matter now. (*He turns to go to the door.*)

**Doris**   You'd better stop right there, Douglas! (*She grabs a paper knife.*)

**Douglas** *is at the door.*

**Douglas**   How very fitting, how very apt. My entire thesis is confirmed, out comes the flick-knife, the switch-blade.

**Doris**   Douglas, it's a paper knife.

**Douglas**   Rich or poor, this is where drugs will inevitably lead you. It will be gang colours, automatic assault rifles and shoulder-held missile launchers next. Goodbye, Miss Wallis. I am sorry for you.

**Doris**   Grab him, Peggy. (*She drops the knife, leaps at him and grabs him.*)

*But* **Douglas** *spins her round and pins her to the wall. During the following,* **Peggy** *discreetly gets something out of her handbag.*

**Douglas**   Don't be a fool, madam! I was eight years a soldier . . .

**Doris**   Peggy!!

**Peggy** *coshes* **Douglas**, *who falls to the ground, senseless, by the sofa.*

**Peggy**   Oh, my God!

**Doris**   Oh, my God. (*Approvingly.*) Nice move, Peggy. I had no idea you carried a cosh. (*She grabs the envelope, checks it.*)

**Peggy**   My mother makes me.

**Doris**   And quite right too. Thank you very much, Douglas, and, incidently, when you wake up you're sacked.

**Peggy** (*kneeling beside* **Douglas**, *stunned*)   He's dead.

**Doris**   He can't be.

**Peggy** (*very upset*)   He is.

**Doris**   The bastard.

**Peggy** (*suddenly she screams hysterically*)   Ahhhhh! What have I done, what have I done? I've killed him! Why didn't you tell me you took drugs, why didn't you say?

**Doris**   Come on, Peggy! Calm down, love, calm down. We're in this together, we'll work it out. (*She hugs her.*) We've got plenty of time, we'll make a plan. Yes, that's it, we'll make a plan. Nobody knows about this, nobody's coming to get you . . . Nobody's coming to get you.

*The door intercom buzzer sounds. They both jump mightily. Both scream.*

**Peggy**   Save me, Doris, you've got to save me, I don't want to go to prison . . .

**Doris**   Nobody's going to prison, stay calm, stay calm. (*She crosses to the intercom, gingerly answers it.*) Hallo . . . (*To* **Peggy**.) It's the pizzas. (*Into the intercom.*) I love you, but we don't really want them any more, we . . . Oh, all right, the front door's broken, come on up. (*To* **Peggy**.) Can you believe it, he wants his money . . .

**Peggy**   But . . . but . . . if he comes in here, he'll see . . .

**Doris**   Don't be stupid, he's not coming in here, is he? You've got to calm down, take this money and meet him at the stairs and pay him . . .

**Peggy**   Well . . . No, I can't.

**Doris**   You've got to, everything must be as normal as possible. Now we're going to get through this together, Peggy. So take some money, go outside and pay the pizza man . . . and don't mention the corpse.

**Peggy**   Right.

**Peggy** *reluctantly takes her handbag and goes out.*

**Doris** *takes the envelope and hides the drugs under the typewriter. Suddenly all the lights go out.* **Doris** *screams in shock in the darkness. She lights a lighter and finds her way across to the candelabras on the sideboard. She begins to light them.*

**Peggy** *appears at the door, laden with pizzas.*

**Doris** *(peering)*   Is that you, Peggy?

**Peggy** *(with a shaky voice)*   Yes, it's me . . . the lights have gone out.

**Doris**   I know that, Peggy.

**Peggy**   It must be a main fuse, the whole building seems to have gone, the emergency lights are on in the stairwell.

**Doris**   Well, it's nice to know that some misfortunes are not exclusive to me.

*She has all the candles going, the light is dim and flickering.*

**Peggy** *(laden with enormous pizza boxes)*   I've got the pizzas.

**Doris**   I'm not really hungry anymore. We have to do something with this body.

**Peggy** *(weeping on her shoulder)*   How . . . there's people in the street, on the stairs, we'll be caught, I know we'll be caught.

**Doris**   Well, if we can't get it out, we've got to give it a good reason to be here . . .

**Peggy** *(trying to think)*   Well . . . well . . . he came to check something about your accounts.

**Doris**   Yes, not bad as far as it goes, but it doesn't explain why he's dead, does it?

**Peggy**   It's my fault, Doris, I killed him, I should take the consequences. What . . . what if I cosh you as well, to prove you weren't involved, then call the police and tell them I went mad?

**Doris**   I don't know if you noticed, Peggy, but the last time you coshed someone they ended up dead.

**Peggy**   Well, I could be gentle.

**Doris**   No, I don't want you to.

**Peggy**   Well, what if I tied you up?

**Doris**   Yes, good thinking, Peggy, not bad, but it's got to look like he was the aggressor. Yes, that's good actually, Peg. Now come on, tie me up, we'll do it here.

**Peggy**   Have you got any rope?

**Doris**   Yes, loads in the bedroom.

**Peggy**   Good. Why?

**Doris**   Never mind about that now . . . I'm scared of fires, it's for escaping, now go and get it. It's in the wardrobe, Peggy, and there's a set of handcuffs under the pillow, bring those as well.

**Peggy**   Right.

**Peggy** *goes into the bedroom.*

**Doris** *sits in the chair up stage, facing the audience.*

**Peggy** *returns with rope and handcuffs.*

**Doris**   Now, we've got to get the plot straight. These are the basics, Peggy, OK? We plant the coke on his corpse so that we can say he came round to blackmail me, and in the process ties me up.

**Peggy**    But, Doris, none of these things happened.

**Doris**    I know that, Peggy, but he's not here to deny it, is he? Now tie me up!

**Peggy** *reluctantly begins to do it.*

**Peggy**    I still don't see . . .

**Doris**    God, you're so thick sometimes, Peggy. Listen, he's tied me up, right? He's threatening me with blackmail OK? You return, having popped out for some hubris to put on the pizzas . . . there's a struggle, during which you triumph, all right? It's just our word, there's nobody else to tell a different story, we'll get away with it. Tighter, Peggy, it has to be convincing.

**Peggy** (*struggling*)    I'm doing my best, Doris . . .

**Doris**    Ow! Yes, that's tight enough, I can't move.

**Peggy**    There, that's pretty good, I was a Girl Guide, you know.

**Doris**    Fascinating; handcuffs. Now get the coke from under the typewriter, I hid it there. Put it in his pocket and then you can ring the police . . .

**Peggy** *gets the envelope. She returns to* **Doris**.

**Peggy**    I'm scared, Doris.

**Doris** (*gently*)    Don't be scared, Peggy, I'll look after you. Really, Peggy, I mean it. I'll always protect you. Now just put the package in Douglas's pocket . . .

**Peggy** *puts it in* **Doris**'s *pocket.*

No, Douglas's pocket, Peggy, watch my lips, darling. Put the drugs in Douglas's pocket . . .

**Peggy** *is still tightening the ropes.*

Put the drugs in Douglas's pocket.

**Peggy** (*gently, but straight into* **Doris**'s *face*)   So, I can't
act, can I?

**Doris**   What?

**Peggy**   So you don't think I can act.

**Doris** *screams suddenly. In the flickering half light* **Peggy** *tears
off her brunette wig; underneath she is blonde.*

(*Shouting in* **Doris**'s *face.*) Viper! Slut! Filthy cockroach!!
You have no human heart, you cannot feel, your soul is
the soul of a witch. It is rotten, cold and dead and you
must die! You're poison, do you hear me?! Bitter, bitter
gall!

**Peggy** *is Trudi Hobson; she now becomes her, turning before our
eyes into an eccentrically mannered actress. Her walk changes into
the slightly showy elegance of those who value their dance training,
no matter how many years ago it was. Her accent becomes the
casual but terribly refined drawl of those who have been taught how
to speak properly. She pushes her wild blonde hair off her forehead.
The quiet, mousy* **Peggy** *has completely vanished. Although she
will continue to be called that.*

Yes, darling. It's me. The silly cow you said couldn't act.
Well, I've acted pretty well the last six months, haven't
I, darling? (*She walks to the door.*) I'll just make us more
cosy, shall I? Wouldn't want to be disturbed, would we?
Now, I can pop the fusette back in so you can take a
really good look at who I am.

*She steps outside for a moment.*

*The lights come back on.*

**Doris**   This isn't possible.

**Peggy** *enters.*

**Peggy**   That's theatre, love. The art of the not-
possible, a wonderful world of make-believe which we,

the actors, make you believe in. Oh, it's easier than you think when one puts one's mind to it. A good cossie and wig, impeccable references forged by a sweet, sweet prop master I know. I offered maximum enthusiasm for minimum salary and you fell for it.

**Doris**    But it's . . . it's so totally out of proportion.

**Peggy**    Out of proportion? Darling, you ain't seen nothing yet. The play isn't over.

**Doris**    What are you going to do?

**Peggy**    Destroy you, my dear. I swore from the very first moment, win or lose, I would bring you down. Oh, it hasn't been so very arduous. Seven hours acting, three days a week. At Rose Bru' we thought nothing of improvising through the night; all we needed was a bottle of cheap plonk, a fragment of Strindberg and we were in Heaven.

**Doris**    You're mad, totally raving barking out of your ruddy tree!

**Peggy** (*pouring herself a drink*)    Well, do you know, I think all actors have to be a little mad, or how could we do what we do? We're so very different from ordinary people, you see. We hurt so very deeply. That is why I had to plan my wicked plan, do you see? I had to do it. The actress in me said I must. And, oh, what a performance! The most wonderful and fulfilling of my career.

**Doris**    There is a dead accountant on the carpet!

**Peggy**    Yes, that's a bonus I must say.

**Doris**    Peggy . . .

**Peggy**    Trudi, darling. Peggy is a character, a part; I loathe these young actors who can't distance themselves from their characters, don't you? It's so silly.

**Doris**   Trudi . . .

**Peggy**   All that method rubbish about 'becoming'
someone, well it's just Americanized bollocks, darling, it
really is, absolute Yank wank. An actor acts, for
heaven's sake, it's a job of work and a bloody hard one
too.

**Doris**   Six months, Trudi, six months you've kept up
this bit of 'acting'.

**Peggy**   Well, you paid me, and, besides, I was resting
anyway. Oh, there was a bit of telly around, but nothing
happening in the West End at all. The place is a
morgue.

**Doris**   Six months, I mean, why, for God's sake?

**Peggy**   Oh, I know it was naughty and I shouldn't
have done it, darling; we in the business are always
taught to develop a thick skin where the reviews are
concerned . . . How, I ask? It's absurd – ask an actor to
develop a thick skin? You might as well ask a flower to
develop iron petals . . .

**Doris**   But it was just a comment, Trudi, a bit of
newsprint . . .

**Peggy**   It damn well hurt. I mean, obviously one
knows that all reviews except the sweet ones are
maddeningly silly drivel, the ravings of a lunatic, and
what's more, a lunatic who simply has not taken the
trouble to understand the piece . . . but you are not even
a critic, you wicked woman, you and your kind are no
more than mindless bullies. Can't act!! Can't act, by
God! I've destroyed your life by acting. I've acted you to
the ground. It was I who switched papers on that
repulsive man Skinner so that he took away your equally
repulsive show treatment . . .

**Doris**   Yes, all right, very clever but . . .

**Peggy**   It was I who informed him of your queenly sexuality, in the hope that he might use it against you.

**Doris** (*getting angry*)   Listen, you mad bitch . . .

**Peggy**   It was I who quite deliberately used your envelope full of drugs to send off your accounts.

**Doris**   It was you who killed a man, Trudi! He's lying there in front of the sofa and forgive me but I don't notice him applauding your performance.

**Peggy**   I didn't kill him.

**Doris**   Yes, you did, you coshed the silly old git and he died.

**Peggy**   Oh, don't be absurd. What would Trudi Hobson the actress be doing in the flat of her arch enemy, murdering people? I've never been here, I don't even know where it is . . .

**Doris**   Now come on, Peggy . . .

**Peggy**   Exactly, Peggy! Who's Peggy? A shadow, a figment, nothing more than a performance. Without me she's gone. And I won't be here. So perhaps it was you that killed Douglas . . .

**Doris**   I didn't kill him and you know it. Peggy killed him.

**Peggy**   I say again, who's Peggy? She's fading fast . . . Did I play her? It seems so strange, after all (*Into* **Doris**'s *face.*) I can't act, can I?

**Doris**   Listen, Trudi Hobson, you are obviously deeply and irredeemably mad, but please, for me, make an effort, clutch for a final moment at the coat tails of Mrs Sanity as she scuttles from your mind forever, and understand that I will not be taking your rap.

**Peggy**    But, my dear, I really don't see how you can avoid it. Because when the police get involved, as eventually they must, there will only be you and the corpse left on my little stage.

**Doris**    Whenever the police get involved I'll still be tied up, or perhaps he tied me up after he got killed?

**Peggy** *begins to collect her things.*

**Peggy**    You won't be tied up, I wasn't that good a Girl Guide. You'll worm yourself free eventually, you'll have to. Your answerphone is on and Peggy's last act was to cancel your appointments. You'll either untie yourself or starve. And when you are free again, you'll be all alone with the corpse and the cocaine and it will be your turn to create a convincing performance.

**Doris**    Sid, Eduardo, they know Peggy existed. They'll say Peggy was real.

**Peggy** *is putting the wig back on – preparing to depart.*

**Peggy**    I really can't see either of those two low-lifes getting involved in a murder enquiry on your behalf. And as to the others I've dealt with, I've been careful to do your business strictly by phone. There are very few people who have caught so much as a glimpse of shy, retiring Peggy. Still, you can ring them when you get yourself free, if you can find your phone book, which I doubt, after all, as you've often said in the last month or two, without Peggy you wouldn't know where your arse was to wipe it. Which, since Peggy is a figment of my imagination, doesn't say much for you, you nasty, pig-ignorant bully.

**Sidney** *appears at the door.*

**Sidney** Someone mention my name?

**Doris** (*with enormous relief*) Sidney thank God you're here.

**Sidney** *hovers at the door.*

**Sidney** Well, it's very nice of you to say so, Doris, I had no idea we were still friends. Just come back for my fax machine – always forgetting it.

**Doris** No, Sid, look, she's tied me up.

**Sidney** *advances into the room.*

**Sidney** Well, there seems to be something of an orgy going on here.

**Doris** Sid, you don't understand.

**Sidney** Oh, I think I do, Doris – don't mind me, I'm broad minded, I've travelled. No chance of a 'ménage', I suppose?

**Doris** Sidney, listen to me. Peggy's not Peggy . . .. She's that actress, she's killed Douglas. Look, he's dead.

**Sidney** *sees the corpse which had been shielded from him by the sofa.*

**Sidney** Bugger my bollocks!

**Peggy** She's gone mad, Mr Skinner. She killed Mr Robertson. I had to tie her up to restrain her. Now, I'm just going for the police, so will you please let me pass?

**Doris** Don't let her go, Sidney. Look at her hair, it's a wig.

**Sidney** *peers at* **Peggy**.

**Peggy** Don't you dare touch me, Mr Skinner. Don't you dare.

*He reaches out and plucks off her wig.*

**Sidney**   It's Trudi bloody Hobson.

**Peggy**   Yes, it's Trudi bloody Hobson. I fooled you just as I fooled that literary pigmy over there. Even though, apparently, I can't act.

**Doris**   Oh, shut your face, you stupid mad cow. Sidney, you've got to restrain that woman, she's gone totally berserk.

**Sidney**   Why should I?

**Doris**   What do you mean, why? So we can phone the police and have her locked up in the looney bin for criminally insane actors . . .

**Peggy**   Please, don't send me to the National!

**Doris**   What are you hanging around for, Sidney. Tie her up or something.

**Sidney**   No.

**Doris**   What?

**Sidney**   I'm not going to help you.

**Doris**   Sidney, please.

**Sidney**   I'm going to let Peggy's little plan take its predetermined course, as if I'd never come back for my fax machine. (*He gives* **Peggy** *back her wig.*) No point messing with a good script, is there? Can't go changing the ending just because some old arse like me blunders in from the wings. No, on the whole, I think I shall leave you two witches dancing around your cauldron.

**Doris** (*desperately*)   Sidney, please help me. You've got to help me!

**Sidney**   I'm afraid old Sid the pig can't help you, my saucy darling . . . After all, who's Sidney?

**Doris**   What?

**Sidney** (*walking up to her and straight in her face*)   So I can't act, can I?

**Doris**   Oh, my fucking God.

**Sidney** *now drops his Sid yobbo character. He is an actor, a tough, northern one, Liverpool Everyman or Glasgow Citizen type of thing, strong regional accent. Plenty of leftish, earthy posing, but every bit the 'actor' that* **Peggy** *is.*

**Sidney**   I was bloody superb in that Alan Bleasdale series, but obviously a Tory cow like you working for a Tory rag was never ever remotely going to even try to understand the piece. That wasn't genuine criticism, that was political propaganda.

**Doris** *tries to speak, but is too gobsmacked.*

**Peggy**   You were, Tom, you were quite superb.

**Sidney**   Of course I was. When I played that Bleasdale brickie on BBC 2, I suffered more than any real brickie has ever suffered, I worked harder than any brickie has ever worked! I was every brickie.

**Peggy**   So in many ways you worked as hard and suffered as much as all the brickies in the world put together.

**Sidney**   Well, I think that's what Alan wanted.

**Peggy**   Marvellous text.

**Sidney** (*turning back to* **Doris**)   So there's me taking the collective suffering of the entire building trade on my shoulders, without claiming my full Equity tea-break entitlement, I might add.

**Peggy**    God, you're a trooper.

**Sidney**    And what did you have to say? I got my flipping accent wrong! You stupid cow! His accent was supposed to be wrong! That was the whole point, the poor bastard didn't know who he was! That was what I was trying to say, I mean I really wouldn't have minded if you'd taken the trouble to understand the piece.

**Doris** (*still a bit stunned*)    So you've been working with each other from the start.

**Peggy**    It's my production, I sought Tom out . . . You were marvellous, darling, truly incandescent.

**Sidney**    Aye, well it's worked out bloody well, hasn't it? (*He kicks* **Douglas**.) The death was a bonus though, that'll really stitch the cow.

**Peggy**    Well, exactly. But you really were marvellous.

**Sidney**    No, no, you were, much tougher role. I could just go for laughs, you had to carry the emotion, the content.

**Doris**    And so what's next for the Bonkers Twins then? Two ends of a pantomime Napoleon in *Looney Bin, the Musical?*

**Peggy**    My dear woman, as I have explained, we are actors, we are supposed to be a little mad. And now, sadly, it is goodbye, Miss Wallis, I do hope you enjoyed our performance.

**Doris**    No.

**Sidney**    I was on that building site for an entire morning – I knew those men.

*They are leaving.*

**Doris**    Stop, please. Come back.

**Peggy**   Well, darling.

**Sidney**   I suppose we must.

*They walk back into the room.*

**Doris**   Good. Right, let's just talk about this as adults, what is it you want from me . . . money?

*They bow.*

(*Calling out.*) What! What are you doing? You can't do this to me!!

*They bow again.*

**Sidney** (*to* **Peggy**)   One more, love?

**Peggy**   No, I think we'd be milking it. Drinky time I think.

**Sidney** *and* **Peggy** *leave.*

*There is a long pause.*

**Doris** (*struggling*)   Come back!! Come back, you mad actors . . . (*She struggles again.*) Come back . . . (*With more struggling, she screams dramatically at the top of her voice.*) All right, I admit it, you can act, you can act, you can act!!

**Douglas** *raises his head from the floor and speaks in a huge actor's voice.*

**Douglas**   Act. And what about me, you horrid woman!

**Doris** *shrieks.* **Douglas** *leaps up. He is now not* **Douglas** *at all, but an actor of the old school, a deep velvet-voiced luvvie, who never got to play Lear, a mad, outrageous old ham.*

(*With a huge voice.*) 'Blow winds and crack your cheeks!' (*With a tiny voice.*) 'Tell me not now that Little Nell is dead' . . . (*He walks over and stands over her.*) Isn't that acting, madam! Have I not the muse!

**Doris**    I want my mum.

**Douglas** (*a huge performance*)    Just so have I, a thousand times, yearned for the comfort of a mother's breast, when I recall your cruel jibe, 'Dickhead of the Day'. Twice in the *Preston Clarion* did you give me such a title! 'Ham', you called me! Ham! I, madam, am an actor! I know of no such meat. Noël Coward impressions, I knew the master quite well actually and he would have laughed at the suggestion.

**Doris**    So you're not dead then?

**Douglas**    No, foul woman, I am not dead. I live to taste the sweet knowledge that you thought I was dead, just as you thought I was your accountant, whom Peggy so conveniently found for you. You thought both these things, foul lady, even though, apparently, (*Into her face.*) I cannot act . . .

**Eduardo** *appears at the door.*

**Eduardo**    Happening, what's shakin' slag?

**Doris**    Oh, Christ.

**Eduardo** (*walking in*)    Thought this geezer was your accountant, now he's tying you up. (*To* **Douglas**.) You giving her a portion or what? (*To* **Doris**.) He your toy grandad then? Happening. Anyway, if you two are up for a bit of rumpy-pumpy, I won't keep you, just wanted some dosh for that toot I scored you, I forgot before . . .

**Doris**    Come off it, Eduardo, get it over with, pull your nose off and show me who you are . . . Felicity Kendal?

**Eduardo**    Oh, this is classic, what have you been puffing, Doris? I wish I'd had some, it must be banging good gear, eh, Dougy boy?

**Douglas**    I answer to no such name, young man.

**Eduardo**    Eh? You been blowing and all, have you?

**Doris**    Eduardo, don't tell me you're a real person, you're not an actor!

**Eduardo** *glares at* **Doris**. *Suddenly he drops the wide-boy act and becomes what he is, a beautiful, sensitive, pretentious, young actor.*

**Eduardo**    Actors are real people, you bitch. Just because we're talented and special doesn't mean we don't bleed. People still call me 'that poof off the ravioli ads', because of you. I was making fifty thousand pounds a year when they dropped me. I had to give up my clowning, my mime classes. I am a half-trained mime! Can you imagine the emptiness? I know how to get into the glass box but I can't get out of it.

**Douglas**    Poor boy. How you young lions torment yourselves.

**Eduardo**    Yes, thanks, mate.

**Doris**    This isn't happening.

**Peggy** *and* **Sidney** *enter.*

**Peggy**    I see that you two loves have both had your *coup de théâtre's* then?

**Douglas**    And sweet it was, my dear lady, sweet it was.

**Eduardo** (*anguished*)    I wasn't happy with mine, it was a disaster . . . It wasn't centred, it wasn't consistent . . .

**Douglas**    But, my boy, you were wonderful, wonderful.

**Eduardo**    No, I wasn't. I was crap. I know I was crap,
oh, God, I don't know why I even kid myself that I can
act. It's a joke, a ruddy joke, me an actor?

**Peggy**    Oh, darling!

**Eduardo**    Ha! I know I'm better than any other actor
of my generation, but what the hell does that prove?

**Douglas**    Poor, dear boy, tearing yourself apart
inside. You'll learn, young fellow, you'll learn. Suffering
is part of your apprenticeship . . . (*To* **Sidney**.) I enjoyed
you, Tom, that was a wicked improvisation though,
kicking me while I was down – I nearly grunted.

**Sidney**    Oh, I knew you were too much the pro for
that, mate.

**Douglas**    Ah, yes, playing a corpse is a tough job of
acting. So many young fellows think you just have to be
physically still. Wrong! You have to be brain dead.

**Sidney**    Anyway, pays you back for putting that
tampon in the handbag when we were doing *The
Importance* at Hull, do you remember?

**Douglas** (*laughing*)    God, that's a good story, that one.
The tampon in the handbag in Hull. I don't think
Trudi's heard that one.

**Peggy**    Do you know, I don't believe I have.

**Doris**    Oh, God!

**Sidney**    Well, me and this hell-raising old sod were
playing *The Importance* at Hull, freezing cold winter, no
heating in the dressing rooms. And then one night his
nibs here decides to raise a little Hades. Well, my liege
only goes and puts a tampon in the handbag, doesn't he!?

**Peggy** *shrieks.*

**Douglas**    God, we raised some hell though, didn't we?

**Sidney**    Aye, we supped some decent pints.

**Peggy**    A tampon, priceless.

**Eduardo**    When I'm on stage, I'm dying inside.

**Sidney**    And so you should be at your age. You can raise some hell when you've learnt your flipping craft and not before. If you're looking for an easy life in the theatre, become a bloody agent.

**Peggy**    Oh, don't, mine's a nightmare – ten per cent for bugger all.

*They are all about to tell their agent stories.*

**Doris**    Excuse me, I don't want to keep you, I know you're all anxious to get your strait-jackets fitted but do you mind if I clear up one or two points here?

**Peggy**    Of course, an actor must always encourage audience feedback.

**Eduardo** (*squatting down*)    Perhaps we should workshop it?

**Douglas**    I fear you must count me out if you do, dear boy. I would look an absolute sight in a leotard.

**Doris**    I just want to get the plot straight . . . There never was a Euro job?

**Peggy**    Of course not.

**Doris**    And nobody has stolen my idea for Sky, or told the press about my girlfriends, or faxed Sidney's letter to my boss?

**Sidney**    Props love, ever heard of 'em? The actor is given an empty case, the audience perceive a portable fax machine. That is what makes actors special.

**Douglas**   Hear, hear.

**Eduardo**   Hey, Tom. I think it would have been really good if you'd mimed the case. What do you think, mate?

**Sidney**   Somehow I don't think she would have bought that, son.

**Doris** (*cutting in*)   And no-one's told the police about my little habits, or anything . . .

**Peggy**   Nothing has happened, darling, nothing at all. It was a play, don't you see, you've just been in a play.

**Sidney**   And now the play is nearly over.

**Douglas**   Drinky time.

**Peggy**   Hear, hear.

**Eduardo**   I might join you if there's time, but I like to unwind, alone, for a moment or two after the catharsis.

**Sidney**   Well, yes, a couple of years carrying a spear in laddered tights will knock that out of you, son. But now our audience must applaud us . . . (*He gestures at* **Doris**.)

**Peggy**, **Douglas** *and* **Eduardo** *exit.*

**Doris**   What?

**Sidney**   Oh, yes, the most important part is yet to come. You, Doris Wallis, and you alone, must applaud us all. We must hear your ringing approbation, your heartfelt tribute to actors who, in your humble, ignorant opinion, can act . . . Can you do it?

**Doris** (*woodenly*)   Yes.

**Sidney**   Go on, have a little practice, we don't want to spoil the final moment . . .

**Doris** *claps.*

Oh, come on, I think we deserve more than that.

**Doris** *claps louder.*

Right, keep it going . . . And so ladies and . . . well, lady anyway, it's a small audience, but it's not the size of your audience, it's the size of your performance. So would you, Doris Wallis, please welcome back into your sitting-room Quentin Hopkins who played the part of Eduardo the toy boy . . .

**Eduardo** *enters and takes a bow (with his back to the audience) as* **Doris** *applauds.*

I think one or two 'bravos' might be in order, eh?

**Doris** (*woodenly*)    Bravo.

**Sidney**    All right, son, don't milk it. Kelvin Cruikshank as Douglas Robertson the accountant . . .

**Douglas** *enters and bows.*

**Doris** (*clapping*)    Bravo.

**Sidney**    And myself, Tom Warwick, Sid the editor . . . (*He bows and raises a fist.*) fight the cuts.

**Doris**    Bravo, (*After a pause.*) you wanker.

**Sidney**    And finally, you will be applauding our leading lady, who for the remainder of the evening will be taking over the part of Doris Wallis!!

**Peggy** *enters. She is dressed exactly as* **Doris**, *her hair and make-up are the same, she looks just like her.*

**Doris** *stops clapping.*

**Doris**    What?

**Sidney**   Oh, yes, she said you were going to die,
Doris, die the public humiliation that she did. And you
will, pal, you will . . . tonight your public will watch you
die.

*The door intercom buzzer sounds.* **Eduardo** *answers it.*

**Eduardo** (*into the intercom*)   Hallo . . . (*To* **Peggy.**) It's
the car for *Wogan.*

**Peggy**   Tell them I'll be right down.

*Black-out.*

# Popcorn

## Characters

**Karl Brezner**
**Bruce Delamitri**
**Velvet Delamitri**
**Farrah Delamitri**
**Wayne Hudson**
**Scout**
**Brooke Daniels**
**Kirsten**
**Bill**

The action of the play occurs principally at the Beverley Hills home of top film director Bruce Delamitri

**Time**: the present

## Synopsis of scenes

*Popcorn* was first presented in association with The West Yorkshire Playhouse at the Nottingham Playhouse in September, 1996 with the following cast:

| | |
|---|---|
| **Karl Brezner** | David Leonard |
| **Bruce Delamitri** | Vincenzo Nicoli |
| **Velvet Delamitri** | Emily White |
| **Farrah Delamitri** | Melee Hutton |
| **Wayne Hudson** | Patrick O'Kane |
| **Scout** | Dena Davis |
| **Brooke Daniels** | Elizabeth Perry |
| **Kirsten** | Tamara Letendre |
| **Bill** | Bret Jones |

*Directed by* Laurence Boswell
*Designed by* Neil Irish
*Lighting by* Jon Linstrum

Subsequently presented by Phil McIntyre at the Apollo Theatre, London, on 2nd April 1997 with the following cast:

| | |
|---|---|
| **Karl Brezner** | William Armstrong |
| **Bruce Delamitri** | Danny Webb |
| **Velvet Delamitri** | Paula Bacon |
| **Farrah Delamitri** | Debora Weston |
| **Wayne Hudson** | Patrick O'Kane |
| **Scout** | Dena Davis |
| **Brooke Daniels** | Megan Dodds |
| **Kirsten** | Sarah Parish |
| **Bill** | Richard Laing |

*Directed by* Laurence Boswell
*Designed by* Jane Clough
*Lighting by* Jon Linstrum

**Note**
Please note the following contemporary references:

Oprah (Oprah Winfrey): American agony aunt/chat show host
OJ (OJ Simpson): American star acquitted of the murder of his wife in a televised court case
Roseanne: popular TV comedienne

# Act One

## Scene one

*The lounge room of film director **Bruce Delamitri**'s home in Beverley Hills.*
*The day of the Oscar ceremony.*

*The entry to the lounge and staircase to the bedroom are* SL. *Two pillars stand each side of the* CS *patio doors overlooking the garden. The doors are covered with drapes and practical shutters which are operated by remote control. An intercom is also visible. There is a large glass coffee table* CS, *an ashtray, telephone, paper and pen, stereo, rug and two sofas with furry cushions. A large drinks cabinet* SL *is filled with bottles, glasses etc. including bourbon and crème de menthe. The back of a* TV/video *is visible to the audience.*

**Bruce Delamitri**, *an extremely famous and equally hip film director in his late thirties, and* **Karl Brezner**, *the producer of* **Bruce**'s *films, have been watching a movie clip on the* TV/video. **Velvet**, **Bruce**'s *teenage daughter, sits reading a magazine. As the scene opens* **Bruce** *has been watching the clip with* **Karl**. *The music ends and as* **Bruce** *zaps the* TV *off with a remote control, the* TV *is concealed (perhaps electronically).*

**Karl**  It's a great scene, Bruce. The clip'll play beautifully.

**Bruce**  I know it's a great scene Karl! I made the damn movie! They're all great scenes, but the scene in the cellar is better. That's the clip they have to use.

**Karl**  They don't have to use any scene, Bruce. They are the Academy and it is their party. Forget the clip, worry about your speech. Did you write it yet?

**Bruce**   I'm not writing any speech, Karl, because I'm not going to win any damn Oscar. I'm too good a director. The Academy is there to celebrate anodyne mediocrity. Anyway it'll be a woman this year.

**Karl**   Well whatever, they are not going to use the cellar clip.

**Bruce**   Why the hell not, what is their problem?

**Karl**   The Chair of the Academy says she feels it's overly gynaecological.

**Bruce**   Gynaecological! Did she watch the movie? The girl's private parts are not shown, they are implied!

**Karl**   Even a subliminal vagina is unacceptable on prime time, Bruce.

**Bruce**   Karl ! We do not see her snatch!

**Karl**   Nonetheless, the character Errol stares up it.

**Bruce**   Ironically.

**Karl**   An Oscar telecast is not a medium suited to irony, Bruce. The committee are worried people will just think it's dirty.

**Bruce**   Dirty! How can it be dirty! Errol stares up Conchita's private parts in a manner that clearly implies an ironic juxtaposition, didn't you get that?

**Karl**   Bruce, I just produced the movie, who cares if I get stuff.

**Bruce**   It's so obvious! The very next shot is the private parts' point of view!

**Karl**   Christ Jesus, Bruce, get real. This show goes out to over a billion people the vast majority of whom would be surprised to hear that a vagina can even have a point of view, let alone get it aired on prime time . . .

**Bruce**  Of course a vagina can have a point of view! Not intellectually, obviously, but cinematically.

**Karl**  Errol's leering mug.

**Bruce**  Yes, except Errol's face is not leering, it's shrugging and that's the point. The character Errol is indifferent. This is all in a day's work for the guy. He's almost – bored! This is just a job. An American job.

**Karl**  Bruce, be realistic! Shooting women in the guts then rummaging about inside them for hidden drugs is not a common occupation.

**Bruce**  Killing is and that's the point I'm making! Being a killer is a career option in America, like teaching or dentistry.

**Karl**  Maybe not quite as common. Bruce, be fair, the Academy are taking a lot of heat here. Yours has to be the most controversial nomination in history. 'Ordinary Americans' was about a young couple out on a killing spree and as you are well aware there is currently a very similar young couple on a very similar . . .

**Bruce**  Yeah I know, I know! The fucking Mall Murderers. My babies! Every time their crimes are reported the story gets illustrated with a still from my movie! So who's making the association? The psychos themselves? I don't think so. Copy-cat murders for Christ's sake! The lowest, cheapest shot of a hysterical media. Weren't there any sickos around before we had movies?

**Karl**  Society is more violent that it used to be Bruce, that's a fact.

**Bruce**  Exactly, and someone has to get blamed. The politicians won't take the heat! So who gets it? Us, the messengers, the artists. Well, artists don't create society,

they reflect it and what's more I'm going to tell them
that if I win tonight, which I won't, but if I do and I
won't, I will.

**Velvet**   Yeah, and you'll sound like a totally pompous
jerk.

**Bruce**   Hey, principles may not mean much to you
and your brain-dead pals young lady but I come from
the generation that dared to care.

**Velvet**   Please, Dad, I just ate lunch.

**Bruce**   Didn't your mother pick you up yet?

**Velvet**   Yeah, I'm a hologram.

**Bruce**   Your mother is supposed to pick you up.

**Velvet**   Well, I'm so sorry to be still infesting your
environment, Dad! Jesus, the stuff I'm going to be telling
Oprah one of these days.

**Karl**   Why don't you take Velvet to the Oscars
tonight, Bruce? Father and daughter, best pals despite
nasty, messy divorce. Nice family image. Respectable.
Could play well in the press.

**Bruce**   I don't want to look respectable, I'm a
maverick.

**Velvet**   He wants a free hand to pick up some
slutlet at the Governor's ball.

**Bruce** (*to* **Karl**)   Fifteen years old, do you like
that?

**Karl**   Generation X, Bruce.

**Bruce**   Generation ex-tremely fucking irritating.
I'm working here, Velvet.

**Karl**   If you win an Oscar tonight –

**Bruce**  Which I won't.

**Velvet**  I think you will.

**Bruce**  Well, I should honey, which is why I won't.

**Karl**  No, but if you do –

**Bruce**  I won't.

**Karl**  Well, whatever, if you do you have to be nice. Smile, maybe cry a little, whatever, above all don't mention the Mall Murderers. Hollywood does not forgive a party pooper.

**Bruce**  Which is why the intro clip is so important. It's got to have balls.

**Karl**  So now this vagina has balls as well as a point of view, quite some pussy.

**Velvet**  You're disgusting Karl.

**Karl**  Look, they are not going to use the cellar clip; I tried, I failed.

**Bruce**  Well, did you suggest the shoot-out in the bank?

**Karl**  I did, yeah. And they have problems with that too.

**Velvet**  I like that scene, it's cool.

**Bruce**  What kind of problems?

**Karl**  A woman sticking a broken bottle in a guy's dick type problems.

**Velvet**  Great scene, she just totally perforates that rapist asshole.

**Bruce**  Exactly! The female protagonist is clearly depicted in a befittingly empowering light.

**Karl**   After we have seen her befittingly roughed up and taken a long look at her befittingly beautiful tits.

**Bruce**   Her revenge means nothing, unless we see her vulnerability . . .

**Karl**   *Her tits, Bruce, you can't show tits on network TV!*

**Farrah** *enters.* **Bruce***'s nearly divorced wife. A Hollywood survivor in her late thirties.*

**Farrah** (*to* **Velvet**)   Hiya baby . . .

**Karl**   Farrah . . .

**Farrah**   Oh please Karl. Big night tonight, Bruce. I hope you got a new tuxedo. Remember I cut your Armani into little pieces after I caught you stroking Pussy Woman at the last *Batman* première.

**Velvet**   Cat Woman, Mom.

**Farrah**   I know what I'm saying.

**Bruce**   Noon, Farrah, the deal was noon.

**Farrah**   What? It's such a pain to have your own daughter in the house an extra couple of hours.

**Bruce**   We were supposed to discuss the damn divorce.

**Farrah**   I'll stop by tomorrow.

**Bruce**   What was wrong with today?

**Farrah**   I saw my hypnotherapist. It's an inexact science, Bruce. You can't put deep trauma on hold. When the truth emerges you need to be there.

**Velvet**   Mom's uncovered memories of childhood emotional abuse. She was deprived of attention.

**Bruce**   No, you mean people didn't like her.

**Velvet**    Maybe that's why you and Dad didn't make it, Mom, maybe you're a paranoid dysfunctional incapable of sustaining relationships.

**Farrah**    The reason I can't sustain a relationship with your father, Velvet, is because he is an asshole.

**Velvet**    You used to love him.

**Farrah**    I used to love the Osmonds.

**Bruce**    Hey, if I'm an asshole at least I got that way without any help. Childhood emotional abuse? Jesus, Farrah!

**Farrah** (*to* **Velvet**)    Can you believe your father? I tell him I've been emotionally abused, what does he do? Emotionally abuse me.

**Bruce**    That's right! We should be celebrating. Farrah just got her self indulgence licence. Now you can drink, you can take drugs, you can fuck up your life completely and none of it will be your fault.

**Velvet**    You two make me want to puke.

**Bruce**    Beautiful, Velvet, I get so proud when you talk that way.

**Velvet**    Well, you raised me, if you can call it that.

**Bruce**    So now I've got bitches in stereo. You hear that, Farrah! So now she's off the hook too, you blame your parents, Velvet blames us, how many generations before the buck stops?

**Karl**    Hey, Bruce, Farrah, you know I hate to break up this . . .

**Farrah**    Well don't, Karl. I'll go when I want to. This is California, remember. Half this house is mine. (*To* **Velvet**.) Get me a drink, honey.

**Velvet**  Mom you said you weren't going to drink today . . .

**Farrah**  Hey, give me a break, will you? Can I help it if I have an addictive personality?

**Velvet** *goes to the drinks cabinet and pours* **Farrah**'*s drink.*

**Bruce**  You hear that, baby, it's not your mother's fault, her personality's to blame. Nothing is anybody's fault. We're all victims, alcoholics, sexaholics, shopaholics . . .

**Velvet**  Hey leave me out of it.

**Bruce**  We are losing more kids a year to violence than we did in the Vietnam war and what are they blaming! My fucking movies!

**Velvet** *hands the drink to* **Farrah**.

**Farrah**  Well, surprise surprise, what does he finally get back to? His movies of course. We start off talking about my trauma but in the end we get back to Bruce Delamitri's movies. The only thing on earth that matters. Well the best thing about divorcing you, honey, is that I get not to have to hear about your movies ever again. Forget the drink. (*She puts the glass on the table.*) Come on Velvet.

**Velvet**  Good luck tonight Dad. Even if you don't win –

**Bruce**  Which I won't.

**Velvet**  – and even if you are a pompous jerk –

**Bruce**  Which I'm not.

**Velvet**  – you're still emotionally relevant to me.

**Bruce**  Thanks, baby.

**Farrah**   Come on, Velvet.

**Farrah** *and* **Velvet** *exit.*

**Bruce**   Velvet's a good kid.

**Karl**   She should be, the money you've spent on her.

**Bruce**   Hey, love has no budget.

**Karl**   Beautiful Bruce.

**Bruce**   OK. So they won't use the cellar clip or the bar room. How about the shoot-out in the bank? That's a nice punchy scene.

**Karl**   Maybe. We can only ask. I'll make the call.

**Karl** *picks up his mobile phone.*

*Black-out.*

**Bruce** *and* **Karl** *disappear.*

*Instantly, through the darkness we hear a screaming shout . . .*

**Wayne** (*off*)   You are one dead mutha!


**Scene Two**

*The shout is followed by the sound of gun fire and screams in the darkness.* **Wayne** *and* **Scout** *appear, carrying machine guns, hysterically elated.*

**Wayne** (*shouting*)   I love you, sugar pie!

**Scout**   I love you too honey.

**Wayne**   Oh my God, shooting people makes me so horny! I want to do it to you sugar, I want to screw you till your teeth rattle.

**Wayne** *pulls* **Scout**'s *dress up round her waist.*

**Scout**   We are in a bank, Wayne! This is a public place! There are people here!

**Wayne**   No problem, baby doll.

**Wayne** *fires his machine gun this way and that, out into the darkness. We hear screams and sobs.* **Wayne** *stops firing; the screaming subsides to a few sobs.*

**Scout**   Oh Wayne, I surely do love you.

*Black-out.*

**Wayne** *and* **Scout** *exit. The scene disappears.*


## Scene Three

*On another part of the stage a light comes up.* **Bruce***, wearing a tuxedo, stands at a podium in a single spotlight, an Oscar in his hand.*

**Bruce**   I stand here on legs of fire – I want to thank you all. Your indomitable spirit has nourished me and helped me to touch the stars. Helped me be better than I had any right to be. Better than the best which is what you all are. Wonderful people. Wonderful Americans, whose extraordinary, awesome, monumental, heaven-sent talent has made me the artist I am. You are the wind beneath my wings – and I flap for you.

God bless you all, God bless America, God bless the world as well.

Thank you.

*Huge applause.* **Bruce** *disappears. Cut spotlight.*

**Scene Four**

**Wayne** *and* **Scout** *appear out of the darkness.* **Wayne** *carries a large bag. The lights begin to fade up.*

**Wayne**    Ain't nothing like killing, Scout. I done it all in my time, stock cars, broncos, gambling, stealing and I am here to tell you that there ain't nothing to touch the thrill of killing. Yee ha!

*The full lights have faded up and we realize that we are in* **Bruce**'s *lounge room. Clearly this must be a telling moment for the audience as they realize that* **Wayne** *and* **Scout** *are real and are in* **Bruce**'s *home.* **Scout** *is staring about in child-like wonder.*

**Scout**    Don't shout so, Wayne. I was just enjoying the early morning peace. Wasn't it a beautiful dawn? Isn't this a beautiful home?

**Wayne**    Sure it's beautiful, sugar pie. The man who owns it is a king in this town. Why I guess he's damn near as famous as we are!

**Scout**    Ain't it something? Don't you just love the furry cushions and glass coffee tables and all?

**Wayne**    You know why they have those glass coffee tables, precious? You want to know why they have them?

**Scout**    So's they can put their coffee down.

**Wayne**    No it ain't, baby. It's so they can get underneath and watch each other take a dump, yes it is honey, I read that, it sure is.

**Scout**    That is not so Wayne! It is just not so and I do not want to hear about it. Just when everything is nice

you have to start on about people going to the bathroom
on their coffee tables.

**Wayne**   That's the real world honey, it's weird. People
are weird, they ain't all nice like you and me. I feel good
baby doll, do you feel good?

**Scout**   Yeah, I feel good Wayne.

**Wayne**   I always feel good after I kill a whole bunch of
muthas. You know what Dr Kissinger said, baby.

**Scout**   You didn't tell me you'd seen no doctor,
honey.

**Wayne** *sits on a sofa and puts his feet up on the cushions.*

**Wayne**   He wasn't no real doctor, he was the
Secretary of State. A powerful man, killed a whole lot
more people than you and me ever will and he said
power was an aphrodisiac, which means it gets you
horny.

**Scout**   I know what an aphrodisiac is, honey.

**Wayne**   Well you ain't never going to get more power
over a person than when you kill them so I guess killing
is an aphrodisiac too.

**Scout**   I guess so honey – you get your dirty boots off
that couch and mind out for all that blood on your
pants. This is a nice house and I'll bet the people who
own it are real nice people and we don't want to get no
blood on their couch.

**Wayne**   They ain't necessarily so nice, pussycat.
Besides the blood is dry. Blood dries real quick on
account of it congeals. You know what honey? If your
blood didn't congeal you could die from just one little
pin prick.

**Scout**   I know that Wayne.

**Wayne**   And you would be what is known as a homophobic.

**Scout**   Honey, a homophobic is a person who does not approve of carnal knowledge between a man and a person of the same sex. I believe you're thinking of a haemophiliac.

*Wayne gets up; suddenly he is sullen, sinister.*

**Wayne**   Is that so?

**Scout**   Yes, honey, it is.

**Wayne**   Is that so?

**Scout**   I believe so, honey.

*Wayne grabs her in sudden fury, his fist clenched, ready to strike.*

**Wayne**   And what d'you call a woman whose mouth is too damn smart, huh? A woman with a busted fucking lip, that's what.

*He pushes her to the ground.* **Scout** *screams.*

**Scout**   No! Please, Wayne, don't!

*Wayne drops to his knees, straddled across her and grabs her throat, fist raised.*

**Wayne**   You think I'm dumb, sugar? Is that it? Huh! Maybe we'd better see if your blood congeals!

*Scout screams in terror. For a moment it seems that* **Wayne** *will beat her. Instead he kisses her passionately. After a moment,* **Scout** *returns the kiss and embraces him.*

**Scout**   Oh, honey, you scared me.

**Wayne**   I know that, cotton candy. I love to scare you because you're just like a little bird when you're scared.

*They are both still on the floor.* **Wayne** *is beginning to kiss his way down* **Scout**'s *body.*

You like to live in a house like this, cotton candy?

**Scout**   Oh yeah, sure. Like I'm ever going to get the chance.

**Wayne**   We're living in it now, ain't we, honey? I'll bet they've got a real big old bed up them stairs. Stairway to heaven. How about it, cherry pie? How about we go upstairs and make some noise?

**Scout**   I ain't doing no nasty in no strangers' bed Wayne – could be we'd catch AIDS or something.

**Wayne**   You can't catch AIDS offa no sheets . . .

**Scout**   If they're dirty sheets, if they're stained.

**Wayne**   Honey plum, these people are millionaires, billionaires even. They ain't going to have no stained sheets. Besides which even if they did you couldn't catch no AIDS off them unless you put them in the liquidizer and injected them directly into your body! Now I bet these people have satin and silk and I do not often get the chance to fuck my little girl on satin and silk.

**Scout**   We do not . . . (*She checks herself and spells it out.*) F-U-C-K, we make love and I don t care if you're coming at me from behind in the rest room of a greasy spoon, it's still making love and if it ain't making love we ain't doing it no more because I do not fuck.

**Wayne**   You're right honey, I stand corrected. And right now I'm just about ready to make love your brains out. So come on honey – let's have us a party. I'll bet they've got a water bed and a mirror on the ceiling and everything – you know something, baby girl? When I get a hold of your ass, I guess I wouldn't let go of it to pick up a hundred dollar bill and a case of cold beer.

**Scout**   Oh Wayne, you know I can't resist your sweet talking.

**Wayne**   Well you don't have to, honey. Get your juicy sex muffin up here.

**Scout**   Don't call it a muffin . . . (*And improv lines.*)

*They exit up the stairs.* **Wayne** *takes his bag with him.*

*The lights stay up. There is a long pause after which –*

**Bruce** *and* **Brooke** *enter. They are still in their evening dress from the Oscar ceremony.* **Brooke** *carries a bag,* **Bruce** *his Oscar which he places on the coffee table.*

**Bruce**   I still can't believe my luck. I win an Oscar, and I get to meet Brooke Daniels all on the same night.

**Brooke**   Oh please, Bruce, get real.

**Bruce**   No, I mean it. I'm a fan. I've wanted to meet you ever since I saw the *Playboy* spread, it was wonderful.

**Brooke**   Thanks – again. I don't seem to be able to get away from that. I do acting too, you know.

**Bruce** (*unconsciously dismissive*)   Yeah yeah, you said – so what can I get you? More champagne? The night is young.

**Brooke**   You certainly know how to party, Bruce, it's nearly seven a.m.

**Bruce**   What! Jesus! My wife will be here at ten.

**Brooke**   Your wife? I thought you were divorced.

**Bruce**   Practically. That's why she's coming round, business stuff.

**Brooke**   Oscar at night, alimony in the morning, life in the Hollywood fast lane.

**Bruce**    She enjoys making my life uncomfortable.

**Brooke**    Oh well – I guess we still have a couple of hours

*There is a significant pause.*

**Bruce**    I wasn't planning on going to bed – to sleep I mean.

**Brooke**    Nice table.

**Bruce**    I like it.

**Brooke**    I can think of a good use for it.

**Bruce**    Help yourself.

**Brooke** *takes some cocaine out of her bag and begins to chop it up on the table, on which now stands the famous statuette.*

**Brooke**    Just to keep you bright and cheery for your wife. First time I ever did drugs with Oscar looking on; I hope he doesn't disapprove.

**Bruce**    Hey, who cares if he does, that little eunuch is mine now. I own him.

**Brooke**    You sure do. (*She snorts a big line of cocaine.*)

**Bruce**    OK, so we're partying! (*He closes the shutters and turns the stereo on.*) I'll get some glasses.

**Brooke**    You know the one thing I didn't like about 'Ordinary Americans'?

**Bruce**    What?

**Brooke**    The sex scene.

**Bruce**    What are you, a nun? That was the sexiest scene I ever made. I edited it with a permanent hard-on.

**Brooke**    Sure it was sexy – but it wasn't true, everything else in the movie was so real. The guns, the

attitude, the blood all over everything – why couldn't
the sex be real too? The only place over-acting is still
encouraged is in sex scenes. Did you ever see *Nine and a
Half Weeks*? Jesus you only had to tap that woman on the
shoulder and she had an orgasm. Why can't the sex be
convincing? Convincing is sexy. Girls wear pantihose,
you know, not stockings, when they get laid they have to
take off their pantihose. I never saw a girl take off
pantihose in a movie.

**Bruce**    That, I'm afraid, is because pantihose is not
sexy. It is impossible to remove pantihose in a sexy
manner.

**Brooke**    You think so?

**Bruce**    I know so, it cannot be done.

**Brooke** *snorts up the last of the lines and stares at* **Bruce** *for a
moment. She stands before him and begins to dance.*

**Brooke**    You want to bet?

**Bruce**    What are the stakes?

**Brooke**    I'll tell you if I win.

*The music plays.*

**Brooke***'s hands are on her thighs now, massaging the material
of her dress, working it up her legs. She contrives to collect the folds
of the dress about her hips in a bouquet-like cluster, almost as if
she is wearing a rather flamboyant tutu. In one quick movement,
almost a jerk,* **Brooke** *pulls the handfuls of cloth right up high,
pulling the folds of skirt to just under her breasts revealing all of her
pantihose and some of her bare midriff besides. Her hose is of
course of exquisite quality. High-waisted, covering* **Brooke***'s
whole stomach, ending a few inches below her ribs in a wide,
black, delicately-embroidered waistband.* **Brooke***'s whole lower
body is now on show, from diaphragm down to the stilettos she*

*wears. All encased in sheer black nylon. Above it all she holds her dress in great silky folds.* **Bruce** *is very impressed so far.*

*She hooks her thumbs under the waistband of her hose and pulls the material slightly away from her skin. Whilst still contriving to hold up her dress she begins slowly to pull the hose downwards, until her arms are fully extended. She raises one leg and places her foot on the glass table. The hose which is now pulled down to a few inches below the gusset of her knickers stretches out taut between her thighs, lending the tiniest suggestion of bondage and constraint to her sultry pose.*

**Bruce** *leans forward and undoes her shoe.* **Brooke** *brings her leg back to the ground and with equal balance and elegance raises the other one.* **Bruce** *undoes the shoe.* **Brooke** *kicks off her shoes and stands for a moment on the rug, holding her dress above the half-descended top of her pantihose.*

*In one movement she lowers herself to the floor whilst simultaneously pulling the tights down to her knees. She rolls backwards on to her back, whilst bringing her knees up to her chest. Lying on her back and keeping her knees close to her chest, she rolls the tights right down to her ankles and along her feet until they cover only her toes which point seductively at* **Bruce**. *One final push on the tights and they fall down. She raises herself, picks up the tights, and gets to her feet. She steps towards* **Bruce** *and drops the pantihose into his lap. She switches off the music.*

So?

**Bruce**   So I hope you don't expect me to be that good with my socks. You win. What were the stakes?

**Brooke**   Come here.

*They embrace, but* **Brooke** *breaks away.*

Just let me get some protection.

**Bruce**   You know what, I think I love you.

**Bruce** *frantically undresses.* **Brooke** *reaches down to her bag which is by her feet. Suddenly* **Brooke** *produces a gun from her bag and swings round and pushes it into* **Bruce**'s *face.*

**Brooke**    Touch me you bastard and I'll blow your brains out!

**Bruce**    What the fuck is going on!

**Brooke**    You think just because I've done nude modelling I'm some kind of whore!

**Bruce**    No . . .

**Brooke**    You looked at me and you saw sex, right? From the first second I've just been a piece of meat as far as you're concerned. Well, now you're going to pay!

**Bruce**    Listen Brooke, this is not necessary –

**Brooke**    Get on your knees and kiss my feet!

**Bruce**    What!

**Brooke**    You heard. Kiss my feet!

**Brooke** *is levelling the gun at* **Bruce**; *he is terrified. He drops to his knees on the floor and tentatively kisses her feet.*

I said kiss them don't wipe your nose on them.

*Terrified,* **Bruce** *kisses with more vigour.*

**Bruce**    Look – Brooke, I'm sorry – clearly I misunderstood the situation – now if I've offended –

**Brooke**    Are you scared?

**Bruce**    Yes I'm scared.

**Brooke**    How scared?

**Bruce**    Very fucking – What do you want?

**Brooke**    I – want – a part in your next movie. (*She lowers the gun.*)

*It takes a moment for* **Bruce** *to realize what's happened.*

**Bruce**    What . . . ?

**Brooke**    I'm an actress, I want a part – that was the stake.

**Bruce**    Put away your gun.

**Brooke** *puts the gun back in her handbag.*

(*Furiously.*) You mad crazy fucking bitch!

**Brook** *quickly argues her point.*

**Brooke**    Your movies make people horny and scared. What did I just do to you! Come on, be honest!

**Bruce**    Pamela Anderson makes me horny, Saddam Hussein makes me scared. I'm not going to put either of them in my movie – you made me kiss your feet! At gun point! I ought to call the cops!

**Brooke**    I've sent you fifty letters! Fifty! Did you see them? Did you read them!

**Bruce**    Have you any idea how many actresses and models write to me! I don't see any of that stuff. I have people.

**Brooke**    I guessed you didn't, that's why I decided to do what I did.

**Bruce**    Have you been planning this all along?

**Brooke**    Yes.

**Bruce**    You're fucking insane. I ought to call the cops.

**Brooke**    I made you horny and I made you scared – be fair, I did; you've got to give me a chance.

**Bruce**    Supposing I said it depended on you sleeping with me?

**Brooke** (*after a pause*)    No. I don't screw on a professional basis.

*Again a pause.*

**Bruce**    Pity – OK, I'll give you a screen test, you crazy bitch. Have your agent call me next week. Believe me, there is no chance that I will forget you.

**Brooke**    Thank you, Bruce, thank you very much. I promise I won't disappoint you.

**Bruce**    You can't disappoint me any more than you already did.

**Brooke**    Hey, I said I didn't screw on a professional basis. I already got my screen test.

*After a pause they embrace. Within moments the pent-up frustration bursts and they are writhing together on the couch.*

*They are too absorbed to notice* **Wayne** *enter, carrying his machine gun and bag.* **Wayne** *crosses to the sofa.* **Brooke** *has had her face buried in* **Bruce***'s neck, she comes out and sees* **Wayne***. Obviously she is pretty freaked.*

Bruce – Bruce – for Christ's sake Bruce, behind you!

**Bruce** *looks behind him, sees* **Wayne** *and falls off the sofa in fear, trying to pull up his trousers as he does so.*

**Wayne**    Morning folks.

**Bruce**    Who are you? – Brooke, do you know this guy? Is this part of your joke thing?

**Brooke**    I do not know this man, Bruce.

*There is a very tense stand-off.* **Wayne** *stares at* **Bruce***, then walks over to him while still covering* **Brooke** *with his gun. He stares hard at* **Bruce***, putting his face right up close.*

**Wayne**    I don't believe this. I do not be-fucking-lieve this. I'm actually here, I'm actually meeting Bruce

Delamitri. I can't tell you what a pleasure it is to meet
you sir. I've been planning this a long time. Scout!
C'mon in here and say 'Hi'. Oh yes, this is a real thrill,
sir. This is awesome. Scout, get your dumb ass in here
right now!

**Scout** *enters rather sheepishly. She is, like* **Wayne**, *heavily
armed.*

**Scout**    Hi.

*But* **Bruce** *and* **Brooke** *can only stare in reply.*

We messed up your sheets some – but you know, with
modern detergents there shouldn't be any problem.

**Wayne**    It don't matter about no sheets, sugar. We
can buy more sheets. This is Bruce Delamitri. You are
looking at the man here. The man. I told you we'd get
to meet him, baby, and here we are.

**Wayne** *gestures at* **Bruce**. *He is holding a machine gun so it is
rather alarming.*

**Scout**    How d'you do, Mr Delamitri. Wayne's a real
big fan of your pictures, sir, he's seen them dozens of
times – me too, I like them too but Wayne, he loves
them.

**Wayne**    But I guess you get real tired of people telling
you all that stuff.

*There is a pause.* **Wayne** *and* **Scout** *are acting like
embarrassed fans, except that they are so heavily armed.*

**Bruce**    Do you want money? I have money, about two
thousand dollars in cash, and there's some jewellery . . .

**Wayne**    Mr Delamitri – may I call you Bruce? We
don't want no money. We got money, we got more
money than we can spend and we don't spend nothing

anyway because we steal all our stuff. We just came around to visit with you. Is that OK? How about we sit down? Maybe we could have us a drink? Would that be OK? I like Bourbon and Scout here'll take anything sweet.

**Bruce** *gets the drinks. The others sit, there is a nervous tension. Obviously* **Bruce** *and* **Brooke** *are pretty scared.* **Scout** *turns to* **Brooke** *in an effort to make polite conversation.*

**Scout**   You're Brooke Daniels, aren't you? Yes, you are, I'd know you anytime from all the magazines you've been in – *Vogue* and *Esquire* and *Vanity Fair* – I love all that stuff it's so glamorous and nice – I've been in a magazine too . . .

**Wayne**   Sure Scout, 'America's Most Wanted'.

**Scout**   It's a magazine! Isn't it, Brooke? – Brooke? It's a magazine isn't it? 'America's Most Wanted' is a magazine, isn't it?

**Brooke**   Yes, it's a magazine.

**Bruce** *gives* **Wayne** *his drink.*

**Bruce**   Look – if you don't want cash I have a customized Lamborghini parked right outside that . . .

**Wayne**   Bruce, I just told you we're here to visit. I don't want your damn car. I got a car. An American fucking car, made with sweat and steel, not some wop faggot-built pile of tin shit. A Lamborghini! Bruce I am surprised at you. When you drive a foreign car you are driving over American jobs.

**Bruce** *backs off scared. He gives* **Scout** *her drink.*

**Bruce**   This is *crème de menthe*.

**Scout**   I love cocktails.

**Wayne** *(turning to* **Brooke***)* Why'd you do that *Playboy* spread, Brooke? I mean I ain't saying it wasn't beautiful because it was but hell I would never let Scout do a thing like that.

**Scout** Oh, c'mon Wayne, as if anyone would ever want to see me in *Playboy* magazine!

**Wayne** Sure they would honey, excepting I wouldn't let you do it on account of the fact that my rule is that if a man looks at you with lust in his eyes, I kill him. So if you was to be in *Playboy* I'd just about have to kill half the men in the United States.

**Scout** You're getting there anyway, honey!

**Wayne** Scout's exaggerating, Bruce. So why'd you do it, Brooke?

**Brooke** *is too scared to answer.* **Scout** *knows the answer, she has read it in a magazine.*

**Scout** She did it, Wayne, because being an in-control woman does not mean denying one's sensuality. Isn't that what you said, Brooke? I read that. She didn't do it for men, Wayne. She did it for herself because she is beautiful and there is nothing wrong in celebrating that. It's called Girl Power.

*But* **Brooke** *is still not up to replying, she can only nod, there is another pause. Again it is down to* **Wayne** *and* **Scout** *to keep the conversation going.*

**Wayne** Well I guess that makes me feel a whole lot better about jerking off in the john over it, Brooke. I confess I never realized I was doing such a fine and empowering thing . . .

**Scout** Wayne!

**Wayne** I want to ask Brooke something now, Scout, and I don't want you getting mad at me. OK?

**Scout**    Well it depends on what you ask her, Wayne.

**Wayne**    What I want to ask is how'd those girls in *Playboy* magazine get their hair the way they do? It always looks so damn perfect.

**Brooke** *finally finds a voice.*

**Brooke**    Well – you know, I guess it's just a question of hairdressing really. They use a lot of mousse and they back light it and sometimes they put in extensions . . .

**Wayne**    Brooke, I do not mean that kind of hair.

**Scout**    Wayne!

**Wayne**    Well I want to know! I mean we tried shaving it, sugar, and you just ended up like some kind of damn Mohican with a rash!

**Scout** *turns to* **Brooke**, *mortified with embarrassment.*

But in *Playboy* magazine those girls just have a little tuft like that was all that ever grew. It don't look shaved or nothing. These are adult women! Not little girls, but all they got's a little tuft. How'd they do that?

**Brooke**    Well, Wayne – one has a stylist.

**Wayne** *(hugely amused)*    A stylist! A pussy hair stylist! Now that would be one hell of an occupation. Yes sir, I guess I could get to like that kind of work.

**Scout**    Wayne, that is enough!

**Wayne** *(delighted with his comic thought)*    Yes sir! I'd work weekends and all the overtime the boss'd give me. I'd be saying 'Can I shampoo that for you madam?' I'd work hard and get me my own salon – there'd be a whole row of women sitting reading magazines with little hair dryers on . . . (*He cries with laughter.*)

**Scout** *is furious.*

**Scout**    That is enough, Wayne!

**Bruce** *has found some courage. He picks up an intercom phone.*

**Bruce**    OK, now I've buzzed down to my security guard. He's in the lodge at the gate. If you leave now, he won't hurt you but if you harm us, he'll kill you.

**Wayne**    *He'll* kill me? Well ho, fuckn' ho. (*He cocks his gun at* **Bruce**.)

**Bruce** *stands frozen, holding the intercom phone.*

Bang – Just kidding you, Bruce. You give that guard a call. If it makes you feel better you give that old boy a call.

**Scout**, *still mortified over* **Wayne**'s *comments, turns to* **Brooke**.

**Scout**    Brooke, I am so sorry that Wayne has gotten to prying into your personal stuff. He does not understand that a woman likes to keep her special private places special and private.

**Wayne** *is watching* **Bruce** *on the phone.* **Bruce** *is clearly getting no reply.*

**Wayne**    He ain't answering you, Mr Delamitri. Maybe he can't hear you . . . Here, let's see if we can't get his ear a little closer to the phone.

**Wayne** *takes a knife from his belt and reaches into his bag. He clearly cuts something and then produces a severed ear.* **Brooke** *screams,* **Bruce** *is equally horrified.* **Wayne** *carries the gory ear over to* **Bruce**, *takes the intercom phone and holds it to the ear.*

(*Shouting.*) Hallo! Hallo! Mr Security Guard! – He don't hear so good does he. (*He holds the ear up to his own lips and shouts at it.*) Hey! You hear me! The guy who pays your wages is calling you, you fucking jerk! (*To* **Bruce**.) How much did you pay the guy, Mr Delamitri? Was he expensive? Because if he was you are being ripped off, Bruce. He wasn't worth shit as a guard. He just sat there in his hut with his big dog and we crept up behind him and killed him.

**Scout**    We didn't kill the dog.

**Wayne**    That's what's wrong with this country! People just don't do the damn jobs they're paid for. No wonder we can't get ahead of the Japs. (*He casually drops the ear into the ash tray.*)

**Bruce**    Listen, I don't know who you are but . . .

**Wayne**    Just no count white trash Bruce. We ain't nothing. The only memorable thing I ever did in my life was killing people.

**Scout** (*proudly*)    We're the Mall Murderers. I'm Scout and this is Wayne. We're the Mall Murderers.

**Wayne**    Scout, I tell people that – we're the Mall Murderers.

**Brooke**    Oh God, are you going to kill us?

**Wayne**    Now what kind of question is that? Me and Scout here never know who we're going to kill till we done it.

**Scout**    It just happens. This is so great isn't it? – I mean us all here together, just sitting talking. Because like, Bruce here is Wayne's hero and I've always admired girls like you Brooke, so beautiful and all. 'Cept I can't deny I think it's a shame about all this cosmetic surgery you girls get done. Cause these days you don't know who's really beautiful and who's just a cut-up sucked-out balloon-boobed bitch.

**Wayne**  So what we all going to talk about now?

*After an embarrassed pause,* **Bruce** *has a go.*

**Bruce**  Well uhm – why don't you tell us something about yourself, Wayne . . .

**Wayne**  Now why the hell would a famous man like you want to know about any of my stuff, Bruce?

**Bruce**  Well – I guess, to be frank, from what I know of your – uhm, work, it seems to me that you kill people whom you do not know. – So, I suppose I thought it might be kind of nice to – get to know you.

**Wayne**  Well, OK Bruce. What can I tell you?

**Bruce**  Well – how about you tell me what it's like to kill someone.

**Wayne**  You want to kill someone? Hell man, do it, it's easy, do it.

**Wayne** *takes his pistol from his belt and opens the chamber, he removes all but one bullet from the drum and offers the weapon to* **Bruce**.

Five, four, three, two, and one left for you. Here take it. Come on. One bullet can do a lot of damage.

**Bruce** *grabs the gun and points it at* **Wayne**.

That's right, you could kill me, or Scout here, 'cepting of course if you did, vengeance would not be a long time a 'comin – well, Bruce, you going to kill someone?

*There is a pause while* **Bruce** *decides whether to kill* **Wayne** *or not,* **Bruce** *puts the gun down.*

**Bruce**  I don't want to kill anyone, Wayne. I just wanted to know what it's like.

**Wayne**  Well, hell, man, you might as well say what's

it like to make a movie. It depends, on the
circumstances, on the victim. I'll tell you what it ain't
like, it ain't witty.

**Bruce**  Witty?

**Wayne**    Yeah, like in 'Ordinary Americans', when Mr
Chop Chop and the other guy get the guy's hand and
stick it in the food processor. You remember that scene?

**Wayne** *takes* **Bruce**'s *hand and mimes the food processor scene
from the movie.*

**Bruce**  Yes, I do.

**Wayne**    It whizzed up blood and chopped onions and
stuff all over their suits and the one guy looks at the
other and says, 'Shit, this suit's Italian'. It got a big
laugh. But we knew they have to go to this real swanky
hotel to waste this dude, there ain't no way they're
gonna get into no real swanky hotel with all blood and
chopped onions all over 'em. So they have to go to the
launderette and strip off to their shorts and sit with their
big guns on their laps reading women's magazines . . .

**Scout**    That's my favourite bit when they talk about
hormone replacement therapy.

**Wayne**    But they don't know how to work the
machines, so when they get to the real swanky hotel to
waste the dude, their suits is all tiny like a little kid's suit,
'cause they shrunk. Man, that was one classy scene.

**Bruce**  Thank you.

**Scout**    I don't know how many times Wayne watched
that movie.

**Wayne**    They said it was ironic and subversive in the
*New York Times;* I just thought it was a classic, the way
they kept on wasting people.

*A buzzer sounds.*

Now who's that coming calling? You ain't pushed no alarm button or nothing have you, Bruce? I'd kill you inside of two seconds.

*The buzzer goes again.*

**Bruce**   I think it's my wife, my ex – we have a settlement to discuss – she's very erratic about time keeping.

**Scout**   Farrah Delamitri! My God I would love to meet her. Didn't I read somewhere you wished she was dead?

**Bruce**   I was quoted out of context.

*The buzzer goes again.*

So I leave it, right?

**Wayne**   You've made an appointment, you keep it. I guess she can see your big old Italian Lambor-fucking-homosexual parked out in the drive and I don't want her getting suspicious about nothing.

*The buzzer goes again.*

**Bruce**   Look, surely we don't need to drag my wife into this. I mean –

**Wayne**   Ain't going to drag nobody into nothing, Bruce, you just have her come on up here, do your business like you would anyhow and then she can go.

*The buzzer goes again.* **Bruce** *picks up the intercom.*

**Bruce**   Hallo? . . . Karl! What the Hell are you . . . ? Listen Karl, it's the morning after the Oscars for Christ's sake . . .

**Wayne**   Who is it, Bruce?

**Bruce**   It's my producer, he's –

**Wayne**   Tell him you're sending someone down.

**Bruce** *is about to protest but* **Scout** *points the gun at his head.*

**Bruce**   OK Karl, I'll get someone to let you in.

**Wayne** *puts the guns away in his bag. He also takes* **Scout***'s bullet belt.* **Scout** *is left with her handgun.*

**Wayne**   I'm going to take a nice stroll down to the gate and let Karl in so we can visit with him for a while. Now he don't have to see no guns or nothing but Scout and me are going to be ready and anybody who tries to mess around with us is going to be one dead mutha, you hear? Now you just sit tight till I get back. Scout, honey, you're in charge.

**Wayne** *exits.*

**Scout**   Sit down, Mr Delamitri. I don't want to have to kill you but I will.

**Bruce** *sits on the floor. Again there is an uncomfortable pause.* **Brooke***, terrified but strong, starts to try and get through to* **Scout***.*

**Brooke**   You know Scout, I think I saw that picture of you. The one in 'America's Most Wanted'. I remember – I remember it was pretty amazing. You're very photogenic.

**Scout**   Yeah?

**Brooke**   Sure, you're a pretty girl, you know that? Real pretty.

**Scout** (*coyly*)   Oh, I don't think so.

**Brooke**   Of course you are Scout, and I think you know it too. Except you don't make as much of yourself as you could. Like for instance you have beautiful hair, but you haven't done anything with it.

**Scout**   Well, all blood and bits of brain and stuff got in it when Wayne pumped this guy who was serving me a soda so I had to rinse it through and now it's a mess.

**Brooke**   Well, I could help you with that Scout. Maybe we could do some make up. I bet you'd look like a movie star. Don't you think so, Bruce?

**Bruce**   Yes, Scout is very pretty.

**Brooke**   I bet any agent would love to have a cute little girl like you to work with.

**Scout**   Why would they notice me? I mean I ain't saying I ain't pretty. Wayne says I could have any man I wanted, 'cepting only for as long as it took him to shoot the guy. But there's a heap of pretty girls in this town.

**Brooke**   OK Scout, I'll be straight, you're a celebrity. You're a killer's girl . . .

**Scout**   I'm a killer too.

**Brooke**   Well, sure, but the world is going to know that he made you do it and in the meantime if I make you as pretty as can be . . .

**Scout**   You really think I could be a star? – You mean you'd help me?

**Brooke**   Of course I'd help you Scout, I like you. We could be friends.

**Scout**   That's easy for you to say while Wayne's threatening to kill you.

**Brooke**   Maybe so, but it seems to me that Wayne is always going to be threatening to kill someone so how are you ever going to make any friends?

**Scout**    I don't know. Sometimes I wonder about that.

**Brooke**    Listen to me, Scout. If ever a person needed friends it's you. We could help you, but you have to help us. Don't you want friends?

**Scout**    Sure I want friends.

**Wayne** *enters with* **Karl**.

**Wayne**    Bruce, this here's Karl.

**Karl**    Hi Bruce, having a party?

**Bruce**    Yeah, kind of. This is Brooke Daniels . . .

**Karl**    Brooke Daniels. Well well well. Miss February, I didn't recognize you with your clothes on. That was a great spread by the way.

**Brooke**    Thank you.

**Karl**    I'll bet the nozzle of that gas pump was cold, am I right?

**Wayne** *laughs*.

Who're these two Bruce, or will the answer make me blush?

**Bruce**    A couple of – actors. I saw them in an improv' night out at Malibu – thought I'd talk to them. Might be right for 'Killer Angels'.

**Karl**    Seeing actors on the morning after Oscar night? That is dedication. No offence to you guys, but for me talking to actors is only one step away from slamming my dick in a door.

**Bruce**    I just thought they had, you know, maybe they had the right look.

**Karl**    For 'Killer Angels'?

**Bruce**   Maybe.

**Karl**   Well, I'm just the schmuck who finds the money, but these kids look about as much like psychopaths as Scooby Doo.

**Wayne**   Would you like me to fix a drink, Mr Brezner?

**Karl**   Water.

**Wayne**   Water? – Well OK, Scout, go get a glass from the bathroom.

**Karl**   Not tap water! Christ Jesus! When I drink water there has to have been at least twenty thousand feet of Alpine granite between me and the last person who pissed it. Get me an Evian.

**Bruce**   I don't have any Evian. Karl, what do you want?

**Karl**   Maybe we could talk down by the pool.

**Wayne** *coughs uneasily.*

**Bruce**   We'll talk here. I am busy.

**Karl**   Well, excuse me. I forgot for one moment that you just won an Oscar and therefore are professionally obliged to treat with contempt those whom formerly you have loved and respected.

**Bruce**   Karl, I didn't sleep either. Could we do this another time?

**Karl**   Maybe you didn't see the papers today.

**Bruce**   No I didn't see the papers.

**Karl**   Well, I hate to be the shit delivery boy here, but as predicted, yours is not a popular Oscar choice. Frankly the editorials would be kinder if they'd given it retrospectively to 'Attack of The Ninety-Foot Booby Woman'.

**Bruce**    Who gives a fuck what those parasites think?

**Karl**    We give a fuck, Bruce. It's the violence thing. The *issue du jour*. Newt Gingrich was on the 'Today Show' this morning, he says you're a pornographer and you should not get honoured for glamorizing murderers.

**Bruce**    Can we do this another time, Karl?

**Karl**    *Another time*! If being called a murderer by the entire right wing of American politics doesn't worry you perhaps you would like to recall that we are severely *financially* exposed here . . .

**Scout** *is bored with this conversation.*

**Scout**    Brooke, will you put my hair up like you said you would?

**Brooke**    Uhm yeah, sure, OK . . .

*Rather nervously* **Brooke** *takes her handbag and goes over to start doing* **Scout**'s *hair.* **Karl** *is a little disconcerted but carries on.*

**Karl**    Clearly the Republicans want to make a mid-term election issue out of it. They think they've got a live one and we need to make a plan.

**Scout**    You know what I love, I love the way mousse comes out of the can. How do they get it all in there?

**Wayne**    It expands, honey.

**Scout**    I know it expands, dummy, because it's bigger when it gets out! But I don't know how it happens, it's the same with cans of whipped cream. How do they *do* that! I mean cream is cream, you can't crush it up.

**Karl** *is astonished at these rough-looking people who are so confidently ignoring him.*

**Karl**  Excuse me, did I become invisible? I'm talking here.

**Scout**  Sorry.

**Karl**  Well, you are very far from welcome. We can kiss goodbye to a fifteen on the video release. That's half our rental gone to say nothing of actual bans, particularly in the South. This damn Oscar could kill us. Can you believe that?

**Bruce**  Yeah, sounds bad Karl, let me think about it a while . . .

**Karl** *still can't believe a man as powerful as he is being interrupted.*

**Karl**  It's these fucking Mall Murderers, Bruce. Christ, what kind of pointless sickos are those people.

**Bruce** (*quickly*)  Well you know – I mean, you have to try and see things from their point of view.

**Karl**  What, you mean the point of view of a socially inadequate jerk-off?

**Brooke** *is still nervously working on* **Scout***'s hair.*

**Brooke**  I really don't think that you can dismiss them that easily.

**Karl**  Pardon me, miss, for appearing rude, but that I should give a fuck what you think. Wayne Hudson and that weird, scrawny little bitch he drags around are fucked-up trailer-park white trash nobodies who have mashed potato instead of brains. The sooner they get fried, the better. I would gladly take them out myself.

*There is a pause.* **Bruce** *and* **Brooke** *are terrified at this* *outburst.*

**Bruce** (*laughing*)    Ha ha. Nice speech. You talk big Karl, but you'd never do it, you always end up on the side of the underdog.

**Karl**    Underdog? Those scum? Like I would waste my tears on such maggots. I would piss on their graves and that of their mothers who no doubt were whores.

**Wayne**    You think the Mall Murderers are fucked-up white trash, Mr Brezner?

**Bruce**    He does not think that . . .

**Brooke**    You can't just dismiss them . . .

**Scout** (*to herself*)    Weird, scrawny little bitch?

**Bruce**    He did not mean that! You should hear the way he talks about his wife.

**Karl**    Excuse me! What is this right now? Oprah? Are we having some kind of debate about these filth? Of course they're fucked-up trash.

**Bruce**    Karl! What do you want! I'm busy here, I have stuff to do and you are getting in my face.

**Karl**    What do *I* want! What do you think I want! Look you have to fight this, it won't go away. Get out there today and work the chat shows. Tell the world that these killers are not your responsibility and –

**Wayne**    OK Bruce. I'm sick of this guy now. We have things to talk about.

**Bruce**    Karl, I appreciate you coming round and I'm going to think over what you said, but right now I'm busy OK so . . .

**Karl** (*astonished*)    You want me to go?

**Bruce**   Yes I do.

**Karl**   Because you have stuff to do with these people?

**Bruce**   Yes.

**Karl** *looks at* **Wayne** *and* **Scout** *with distaste. He turns discreetly to* **Bruce**.

**Karl**   Look Bruce, if you want something rough to mess around with you should talk to me. We're in enough trouble. This is dangerous, you're going to end up blackmailed.

**Bruce**   Karl. Go.

**Karl** *is mystified and offended.*

**Karl**   OK, see you.

**Wayne**   See you.

**Wayne** *takes out his gun and shoots* **Karl** *dead.*

**Bruce** (*shouting*)   No!

**Brooke**, *who is doing* **Scout***'s hair, screams, and pulls the hair.*

**Scout**   Ow! You pulled my hair!

**Brooke** (*nearly hysterical*)   I'm sorry!

*The buzzer goes.*

*Pause. Black-out and another buzzer.*

# Act Two

*The action is continuous from Act I.* **Karl** *is dead on the floor. The buzzer is buzzing.*

**Wayne**  Answer it.

**Bruce**  It's going to be Farrah. My wife.

**Wayne**  Answer it.

**Bruce**  I'm not bringing her into this.

**Wayne**  So tell her to go away. But make it good: if she kicks 'n' hollers, you all cross Jordan together.

**Bruce** *stares at the corpse of* **Karl**.

**Bruce**  Why? – Why did you kill him?

**Wayne**  He called my best girl a weird, scrawny little bitch, Bruce. What would you have done? What would Mr Chop Chop have done?

**Bruce** (*shouting in anger*)  I would not have killed him and nor would Mr Chop Chop who is a fictitious character that I invented, you insane bastard!

**Wayne**  I know that Mr Chop Chop is a fictitious character, Bruce. That don't mean he don't exist now does it? You gon' tell me Mickey Mouse don't exist? Maybe you think old Walt's been counting make-believe money all'a these years. Maybe you paid for this house with green stamps.

**Bruce**  Mickey Mouse, like Mr Chop Chop is a – I'm not talking about Mickey Mouse! My friend is dead!

**Wayne**  Because he dissed my baby so stop working yourself up into ten types of asshole and answer the damn door!

**Bruce** *speaks into the intercom.*

**Bruce**    Farrah, I can't see you right now . . . I have a woman here, Farrah! I'm partying! Go away! . . . Well I do care . . . No! Farrah! Don't . . . Don't! . . . (*He puts the phone down.*) She has a key, she's coming in.

**Wayne**    Well, I'd better move old Karl here then. You don't want to be having no discussion about who gets to keep the wedding presents over a dead body.

**Wayne** *starts to drag the body out of the room.*

**Bruce**    And you'll let her go when we're done?

**Wayne**    Maybe. Long as she don't call us no names. Sit down Bruce, relax, make yourself comfortable, you want things to look normal for your wife, huh? Scout, you keep these good folk on a tight lead, you hear?

**Scout**    Okey dokey smokey.

**Wayne** *drags* **Karl** *out.*

I'm sorry I shouted at you Brooke. I didn't mean nothing, it's just you pulled my hair.

**Brooke**    Scout. Listen to me. This can't go on. Sooner rather than later you're going to get caught and the more trouble you cause the worse it's going to be.

**Scout**    We know that Brooke. But Wayne's got a plan. That's why we came here.

**Brooke**    What plan can he possibly have?

**Scout**    I dunno but he's got one. 'I got me a plan hon', he says 'and everything is go'n be just fine.' That's what he said. He has a plan for our salvation.

**Bruce**    His plan is to get you both killed.

**Brooke**    Bruce, would you mind? Scout and I are talking here.

**Bruce** (*ignoring* **Brooke**)    That's how it's going to happen, Scout; the cops will come, Wayne'll fight and you'll both be shot to ribbons.

**Scout**    Well, if that's how it is then it's OK with me, Mr Delamitri. We'll go out together, in a hail of blood, love and glory. Love and glory. Me 'n' Wayne are going get that tattooed on us one day. It's our motto.

**Brooke**    Love and glory. That's beautiful, Scout, really beautiful. Love and glory – and you do love him don't you, Scout? You love him very much.

**Scout**    I love him more than my life. If I could pull down a star from the sky and give it him I would. If I had a diamond the size of a TV I'd lay it at his feet. I got feelings, Brooke, bigger than the ocean, deeper than the grave.

**Brooke**    Wayne needs help, Scout, and if you love him you'll make sure he gets it. Let us be your friend, Scout, let us be his friend.

**Scout**    If they take him they'll put him in the chair. They'll melt his eyeballs when he ain't even dead yet. That's what the chair does t'ya. I read it.

**Brooke**    Maybe it doesn't have to be that way, Scout. Maybe if we bring him in peacefully they'll put him in a hospital. Bruce is a big man in this state, Scout, he can help – let us be your friend, Scout, let us be his. Give me the gun, Scout.

**Scout** *is wistful, she almost seems to be day-dreaming.*

**Scout**    You think I should give you my gun?

**Brooke**    It's best for us all, including Wayne.

**Scout**    If I give it to you, will you be my friend?

**Brooke**    I said I would be didn't I, Scout, and I keep my word. Give me the gun.

**Scout**    OK.

**Scout** *smashes* **Brooke** *in the face with the butt of her gun.* **Brooke** *falls back, bleeding at the mouth.*

(*Shouting.*) I sure fucking gave it to you didn't I, you bitch! You my friend now? You always keep your word, don't you! So now you're my friend! Say it!

**Brooke**, *lying bleeding, struggles to reply.*

**Brooke**    I'm your friend.

**Scout**    Well, I don't want you for my friend, you whore, because you tried to turn me against my man and that is unforgivable! – Maybe you want him for yourself! Is that it? Are you coming on to my Wayne? If you try it, bitch, I'll cut you into pieces! Now sit down, you slut, and wipe your mouth. We got company coming.

**Bruce**    Yes, that's right – Wayne said to look normal – normal.

**Brooke** *staggers, sits down and dabs at her bloodied mouth.* **Scout** *sits down and puts a cushion on her gun.* **Bruce** *sits very stiffly. It is all very stiff and contrived.*

**Scout**    Maybe we should be talking about something – uhm – you know what I heard? The Martians got Elvis. Uh huh. But that ain't the spooky part. The truth is, they took him in '68 and replaced him with a blob – of ectoplasm – in a jump suit.

**Wayne** *enters ushering in* **Farrah** *and* **Velvet**. *He has concealed his gun. For the moment there are no guns visible,*

*although what with* **Brooke** *in an evening gown hiding a
bleeding lip plus* **Wayne** *and* **Scout***'s trashy appearance, and
the stiff poses, the scene still looks pretty weird.*

**Wayne**  Bruce, your wife's here.

**Farrah**  Some party, Bruce. Socializing never was
your strong point was it?

**Velvet**  Didn't you sleep yet, Dad? You are so gross.

**Bruce**  Velvet! What the hell are you doing here? This
is between me and your mom.

**Velvet**  Well I'm so sorry to visit my own father the
day after he wins an Oscar. I mean obviously you'd far
rather party – with – who are these people Daddy?

**Bruce**  Uhm – well, they're friends of mine, this is
Brooke Daniels and –

**Farrah**  Brooke Daniels? Oh pur-lease! *Playboy*
bunnies, Bruce? That is so tacky.

**Brooke**  I was never a bunny, bitch. I was a
centrefold. And actually, I'm an actress.

**Farrah** *notices* **Brooke** *is bleeding.*

**Farrah**  Well either way, sweetie, if this is some kind
of 'S and M' thing and he's been beating up on you, you
make your claim out of his share of our property, not
mine.

*Suddenly* **Bruce** *grabs* **Velvet** *and pushes her to the door.*

**Bruce**  Get out, Velvet. Right now, get out. I don't
want to see you.

**Velvet**  Please, Daddy, don't try and order me
around, it's embarrassing. I'm a grown woman now. I
have made an exercise video.

**Bruce**   What the hell did you bring her here for!
Farrah. Go now! Get her out!

**Farrah**   I brought her here, Bruce, to remind you that
she and I are two and you are one and that should be
reflected in the settlement.

**Velvet** *is viewing the assembled group slightly nervously.*

**Velvet**   Yes, Daddy and this stuff is private – and it's
morning. I mean can't these people just go now?

**Wayne**   Oh there ain't nothing private between me
an' your ol' man, precious. We're his friends, I'm
Wayne and this is Scout by the way.

**Farrah**   Velvet's right, Bruce, your 'friends' should go
now. Just give them their money and . . .

**Bruce**   My friends are staying Farrah, I told you I'm
busy! So get Velvet out of here! Now!

**Farrah**   Bruce what's got into you? You are speaking
about your own daughter! You disgust me, you'd rather
be with sluts and street trash than –

**Bruce**   No Farrah! You don't mean that . . .

**Scout** *wanders into the conversation.*

**Scout**   Mrs Delamitri?

**Farrah** *looks and turns to her with haughty distaste.*

**Farrah**   Excuse me?

**Scout**   Is it true you got so puke drunk one time you
miscarried? That you retched up so hard you done lost
your little baby?

**Farrah**   What did you say?

**Scout**   Well that's what it said in the *National Inquirer*.

**Farrah**    How *dare* you speak to me in that manner! What is going on here Bruce? Is this some kind of dumb divorce tactic? Are you trying to throw me? Because it won't work.

**Bruce**    Please, Farrah, get Velvet out of here. You can have what you want, everything, I swear. Just take Velvet away now!

**Farrah** *finally realizes something is wrong.*

**Farrah**    Are you all right, Bruce?

**Wayne** *laughs. Suddenly* **Farrah** *and* **Velvet** *are very worried.*

**Velvet**    Mom, I think we should do this later.

**Farrah**    I'll have my lawyer call, Bruce. Come on, Velvet, we're outta here.

**Farrah** *makes to leave. But* **Wayne** *gets up.*

**Wayne**    No need for them legal parasites to get involved, Mrs Delamitri. Fuckin' lawyers are eating away at the soul of this country. So fuck 'em I say. Fact is, I'll be handling Mr Delamitri's side of the negotiations from now on. Is that OK with you?

**Farrah**    Come on, Velvet, we'll talk to your father another time.

**Wayne**    Truth is, Mrs Delamitri, Bruce here wants you dead. I heard him say so himself and I have decided in view of all the pleasure your husband has given me in the past, to fulfil his wish.

**Wayne** *produces his gun.*

**Bruce**    For God's sake, Wayne, let them go! You said you'd let them go.

**Farrah**    Bruce! What is going on!

**Velvet**    Daddy, do something!

**Wayne**    You said you wanted her dead, he said that, didn't he, Scout?

**Scout**    I heard it.

**Farrah**    Bruce – are you trying to have me *killed*?

**Wayne**    You don't go saying stuff you don't mean, do you, Bruce?

**Bruce**    It was a figure of speech, Wayne! For God's sake, man, it was a figure of speech.

**Farrah**    Whatever he's offered, I'll double it!

**Wayne**    Bruce, it is not such a big deal. People get killed every few seconds. In South Central LA they're pleased if they make it through lunch. If your balls drop you're a survivor, you're an old man! C'mon, let me waste the bitch, I'll take the rap and you get to keep everything.

**Wayne** *raises his gun.* **Velvet** *screams.* **Bruce** *is desperately trying to talk* **Wayne** *down.*

**Bruce**    Look, Wayne, I said I wanted Farrah dead because I was imagining something that in thought might be nice but in reality is obnoxious. Like have you ever said 'I could eat a horse.' I'll bet you've said something similar now of course you don't actually *want* –

**Wayne**    Are you patronizing me, Bruce?

**Bruce**    No . . .

**Wayne**    You think I don't know the difference between a figure of speech like 'I could eat a horse' and a man who's telling the truth even though he's too gutless to admit it. You hate this bitch, if she'd died in her car coming here today you'd have been dancing a jig.

**Scout**    Sure he would.

**Wayne**    If fate was to take this fossilized Barbie-looking bag of bones out of your life that would be just fine. Well I'm fate. The bitch has met a psycho killer. Ain't your fault, so don't fight it. Watch me drop her and count your blessings.

**Wayne** *raises his gun.* **Velvet** *screams.*

**Bruce**    Don't! Please don't! I don't want her dead, all right! I don't care what I may or may not have said in the past, I'm telling you now, I don't want her to die! And if my opinion means anything to you, which you keep saying it does, I'm begging you, don't kill her. Just leave her alone. Please!

**Wayne** *lowers his gun.*

**Wayne**    OK OK, just trying to do you a favour, no need to get mad.

*Unnoticed,* ***Brooke*** *has been edging towards her bag. Now while attention is centred on* ***Bruce*** *she slips out the gun that she had tricked* ***Bruce*** *with in Act One and jams it against the back of* ***Scout****'s head.*

**Brooke**    Drop your gun right now, Wayne, you sadistic bastard or I'll blow this sick little bitch's brains clean across the room!

*There is a pause.* **Wayne** *is genuinely surprised at the development.*

**Wayne**    Don't you go pointing no gun on my baby now.

*It is a stand-off.* **Wayne** *has swung round and is pointing his gun at* **Brooke***; she is pointing hers into* **Scout***'s head.*

**Scout**   She won't do it, Wayne.

**Brooke**   Oh yeah? I want to kill you so bad, Scout, I can taste it.

**Wayne**   You know, Brooke, if you kill Scout the rest of you will be dead inside of one heartbeat.

**Brooke**   Maybe so, but you love her and you don't love us. Her for us ain't no trade. So drop your gun right now or I drop her!

**Wayne**   Well, I guess what we have here is a Mexican stand-off. You know the thing I always think, when you get these kind of situations in movies. When two guys are pointing pieces at each other and sweating and all, like there's some problem. I always think why doesn't one of them just quit talking and shoot.

*He fires;* **Brooke** *falls down, shot.*

I mean that has to be the sensible thing to do, doesn't it?

**Velvet** *screams. General shock.*

**Bruce**   My God, Wayne! How long is this going to go on?

**Wayne**   Well, it can't go on much longer can it, Bruce?

**Bruce**   Velvet, get some napkins from the drinks cabinet, to stop the blood.

*As* **Velvet** *gets the napkins,* **Bruce** *gets a cushion and makes her comfortable.*

She's got to have a doctor.

**Wayne**   No can do Bruce. Ain't no doctor in my plan.

**Farrah** What? What plan? Who are you? What is going on?

*We hear the beginnings of the sound of a helicopter.*

**Wayne** The plan for mine and Scout's salvation. I guess they should be here by now.

**Bruce** Who should be here?

**Wayne** The rest, Bruce, I know you're a mighty important man in this town but even you can't save us on your own.

**Bruce** Who can? Who is coming to save you?

*The helicopter noise is getting louder.*

**Wayne** Why the cops and the TV cameras and the reporters and the people of America, who else? – Sure ain't gonna be no Seventh Cavalry; this ain't the movies, Bruce.

**Scout** TV cameras! Oh Wayne, I surely do love you . . .

**Scout** *rushes up to the patio doors. The noise of the helicopter is getting louder.* **Scout** *pulls back the drapes. Some kind of lighting effect should occur, ideally light should stream through the glass patio doors, silhouetting the actors as the audience blink in the glare. It is, however, morning, so perhaps a combination of sunlight and flashing cameras.*

**Scout** *excitedly looks out the windows and the helicopter noise crescendos; the lighting should tell us that it is flying past. As the chopper noise fades we hear a chorus of shouts of 'Scout', 'Scout – over here' and a hundred motorized camera shutters. Then a police megaphone: 'Wayne Hudson. Wayne Hudson. We know you are in there . . .'*

(*Exhilarated, shouting.*) Wayne, there's hundreds of them!

**Wayne**   I know that, baby doll, now let's close those doors, huh! We ain't ready yet.

**Wayne** *aims the remote at the shutters and they close. The reporters' voices become muffled.*

**Bruce**   Ready for what?

**Scout**   They are making some mess of your lawn, Mr Delamitri. I sure hope you're covered for this type of eventuality.

**Bruce**   Is this a hostage thing, Wayne? Are we your shield?

**Wayne**   I don't hide behind no woman, Bruce. Where's your damn TV?

**Bruce** *reveals the TV screen.* **Wayne** *laughs.* **Wayne** *puts the TV on. We hear the sound of news reporters as* **Wayne** *switches channels.*

**Reporter's voice on TV**   – standing outside the house of Oscar-winning director Bruce Delamitri where it is believed that –

**TV voice**   – notorious mass murderer Wayne Hudson and his young partner Scout –

**Another TV channel**   – appear to have taken refuge at the home of the renowned film maker who is said to have inspired their killing rampage.

**Bruce** *can't believe what he's hearing.*

**Bruce**   Jesus, they're blaming me.

**Wayne**   I sure hope so, man.

**Wayne** *switches the TV channel again.*

**Another TV channel**   Mr Delamitri, last seen leaving the Oscar ceremony in the company of nude model Brooke Daniels –

**Brooke**  I am a fucking actress!

**Wayne**  Keep it down Brooke, I'm watching TV here.

**Another TV voice**  – leaving a trail of pillage, mayhem and death, murdering indiscriminately in the manner of the fictitious anti-heroes of Bruce Delamitri's Oscar-winning movie 'Ordinary Americans . . .

**Bruce** *is stunned.*

**Bruce**  They're blaming me! Jesus Christ, they are blaming my movies!

**Farrah**  You hear that, Velvet, now he's angry, someone's dissing his movies. Never mind I nearly got shot by the Mall Murderers!

**Velvet**  Mom! Brooke did get shot!

**Wayne**  Well, I guess if you're just going to keep on talking we might as well have the damn TV off.

**Wayne** *turns off the TV.*

**Scout**  I was watching that, Wayne. How come you always get to hold the thing.

**Farrah**  Wayne, you have to let us go, if the cops are here you can't escape and –

**Wayne**  I don't want to escape, Mrs Delamitri. I asked them to come here. I called them.

**Bruce**  You called the cops?

**Wayne**  No, I called CBS, they must have called the cops, but that don't matter none. Me and Scout here are used to ignoring cops.

*The phone rings.* **Wayne** *picks it up.*

Guess this'll be them. (*Into the phone.*) Yeah . . . That's right, this is Wayne Hudson. Mm mm, besides Bruce

Delamitri we got Brooke Daniels who is an actress by
the way and we got Farrah Delamitri who is a Gucci-
wrapped sad sack of silicone and Scotch and their
daughter Velvet, cute as a button, good TV if I have to
. . . No you listen to me . . . Just give me a number right
now where we can talk to you . . . OK thank you, we'll
be back in a little while . . .

*Having taken down the number he leaves the phone off the hook.*

**Bruce**   What are you doing, Wayne?

**Velvet**   Good TV if you have to what? What do you
mean?

**Bruce**   What is your plan?

**Wayne**   Well, I guess a plan to avoid being executed
for murder, Bruce. I mean that has to be a priority for
me and Scout right now.

**Brooke** *gasps from the floor where* **Velvet** *is trying to treat her.*

**Brooke**   You won't get away. You're going to fry, you
bastards.

**Velvet**   This woman needs a doctor.

**Wayne**   Soon, maybe. You got to understand here,
Miss Delamitri, that I don't mind none if people get
dead.

**Bruce**   What is your plan, Wayne, for Christ's sake?

**Wayne**   Well, Bruce let me tell you. As you know,
Scout here and me have committed murder and
mayhem across four states. Now I wish that I could tell
you that every one of those corpses deserved to get shot.
I wish I could say it was like the movies where rapists,
red necks, bad cops, hypocrites and child abusers get
what they deserve but it just ain't so.

**Scout**  They might have been all those things, Wayne. We never knew any of them long enough to find out.

**Wayne**  Well whatever, honey. The point I'm making here is that we are in deep shit. We are going to get caught damn soon now and when we do, like Brooke here has pointed out, we have a higher than average chance of getting fried in the chair. And that, Bruce, is where you come in.

**Bruce**  What do you mean?

**Scout**  Wayne says you're our saviour.

**Farrah**  Give them what they want, Bruce, anything, just give it them!

**Velvet**  Yes, give it to them, Daddy!

**Bruce**  I don't know what they want! Tell me, I'll give it to you whatever it is.

**Wayne**  We want an excuse, Bruce. We want someone to take the blame.

**Bruce**  Someone to blame? What the hell do you mean someone to take the blame? Some kind of magician? Like the whole thing was an optical illusion and someone else shot all those people?

**Brooke** *coughs in a deathly manner.*

**Velvet**  She needs a doctor! You can't just let her –

**Farrah**  Velvet –

**Wayne**  Listen! I did not ask that bitch to threaten my baby! She is in this dire situation by her own choosing, so shut the fuck up because me and Bruce are talking here.

**Velvet**  But, I just think –

**Wayne**   Or maybe I should shut you up for good?

**Farrah**   Not the nose, it's new!

**Velvet** *begins to cry.*

**Wayne**   All of you, I said shut the fuck up!!

**Wayne** *raises his fist ready to strike* **Velvet**.

**Bruce**   Hurt her and I swear whatever you want from me you will never get!!

**Wayne** *rounds on* **Bruce**.

**Wayne**   You'll do exactly what I tell you to do whether I break this bitch's pretty little face or not.

**Velvet** (*sobbing in fear*)   Don't hurt me!

**Scout**   Now, there's no need to go beating up on no little girls, Wayne, it's beneath you.

**Wayne**   This ain't no little girl, precious pie! Kids're born old in Hollywood. Why this little slut must'a spent more money already in her few short years than your sweet momma would'a earned in fifty lifetimes. She deserves a punch in the mouth!

**Bruce**   You'll get nothing from me if you hurt her!

**Wayne** *lowers his fist.*

**Wayne**   I want you to know, Bruce, that I am minding the wishes of my baby here and not you. Because I can assure you that you will do whatever I tell you to do whether I hurt your little girl or not.

**Bruce** (*desperate now*)   And what is it! *What is it you want me to do?*

**Wayne**   I want you to plead on our behalf. I want you to speak up for us and save us from the chair.

**Bruce**    Plead on your behalf. You're crazier than
I thought. You think my word's going to save you
from the punishment you deserve? You're guilty as
Hitler.

**Farrah**    Just do it, Bruce! Why do you always have to
know better?

**Wayne**    Sure we're guilty if by that you mean that we
done all the stuff they say we done, but that ain't the
point is it? Not these days? These days no matter how
guilty you are, you can still be innocent.

**Bruce**    No, from my limited knowledge of
jurisprudence I don't think so.

**Wayne**    Yes. From my extensive knowledge of trial by
TV I know so. For instance like that chick who cut off
that guy's dick right? She was guilty all right, she never
denied it. She cut off that ol' boy's manhood and threw
it out of a car window. Do you see that bitch in prison?
Huh? Is she breaking rocks in the hot sun? No, because
although she was guilty, she was innocent.

**Scout**    That's right: she done it, but she was innocent
and I agree with her. That bastard beat up on her and
he done raped her too. I hope she used a rusty knife.

**Wayne**    Now, Scout, you know that you and me
disagree on this issue. Personally I don't see as how no
woman can get raped by her husband on account of the
fact that he is only taking what's his anyway.

**Scout**    He is such a dinosaur.

**Wayne**    Personally I think that any Mexican bitch
who cuts the dick off an ex-United States Marine who
has served his country, should rot in a hole.

**Scout**    The court agreed with her.

**Wayne**    The court was a bunch of lesbians and faggots
– anyway, whatever, we're getting off the point here.
What I'm saying is, right or wrong, the greaseball bitch
walked free. She done it, she said she done it, she was
glad she done it, but she walked. Guilty but innocent
you see. You can be both in the land of the free, always
assuming that is that you got an excuse.

**Bruce**    But you've just said yourself you didn't even
know your victims, that they were blameless. Are you
suggesting that there is any excuse for mass murder?

**Wayne**    Bruce, there is an excuse for anything and
everything in the USA! What about them cops who beat
up on the black boy and started a damn riot? They was
videoed! You see them doing time? No sir, you do not.
Remember OJ? They said he killed his wife. Turned out
they'd got the wrong victim. The dead chick wasn't the
victim at all. No way, OJ was the victim. He was the
victim of a racist cop, who incidentally also walked.
Nobody gets blamed for anything in this country, *nothing
is anybody's fault*. So why the hell should we take the rap
for what we done, huh?

**Wayne** *picks up the phone and dials.*

**Velvet**    Daddy, there's nothing to discuss! Just say
what he wants you to say!

**Farrah**    Listen to your daughter, Bruce.

**Bruce**    I'm thinking here!

**Wayne** (*into the phone*)    OK. We gon' make a statement
y'hear? We gon' announce our intentions and tell it like
it is, so what we want is a small ENG crew hooked up to
all the stations. Cable too. We ain't giving no exclusive
here. Also they got to have a direct line to the ratings
computer. I want to know just how big a TV star I am
minute by minute. Now I give you my word as a

freeborn American that the TV people get safe passage,
I guarantee they will not be harmed on account of you
are observers, man, we are the action.

**Scout** ENG. That means Electronic News Gathering.
Ain't Wayne smart?

**Wayne** (*into the phone*)  Now I know what you're
thinking, guys. You're thinking 'bout putting a SWAT
team in here. Bunch of damn commandos dressed up as
TV people right? Well forget it, the crew you send me
best be the smallest crew there is. I am talking one
operator and one recordist. What is more they have to
come in barefoot and wearing only their underwear.
Y'hear me? And I ain't talking no baggy long johns or
old ladies' bloomers here. I am talking the kind of jocks
you couldn't hide a nail file in.

**Farrah** Velvet, straighten yourself up and don't get
blood on your jacket, there's going to be cameras.

**Wayne** (*still into the phone*)  Uh huh – Now I'm going to
come down and check every inch of the people you send
and if you flick with me cop, four more innocent people
going to get very dead real soon and it will be your fault;
what is more every TV station in America's gon' see it.
Bye bye now. (*He puts the phone down.*) OK now, we'd best
prepare our statement.

**Bruce** I'm not making any statement with you!

**Scout** Are we really going on the TV, honey?

**Wayne** Yes we are, baby doll, and so's Bruce here
because if he doesn't –

**Farrah** No Wayne.

**Wayne** I may just kill his darling daughter.

**Bruce** We can't address the fucking nation!

**Wayne**   Oh yes we can, Bruce. You are going to announce to the whole of the USA, and believe me it will be because between you and us we got more celebrity than Elvis making out with OJ using Roseanne for a mattress. You are going to tell the whole USA that we are your fault.

**Bruce**   You're insane.

**Wayne**   You are going to say that having met us and talked to us you realize that we are just poor, dumb white trash and you and your glamorous Hollywood pictures done corrupted our po' simple minds . . .

**Wayne** *takes up the bag which contains the severed head and pulls out a bundle of blood stained magazines and newspapers and starts to hand them to* **Bruce**.

You're going to say you admit that your work is – what's it say there Bruce, I highlighted some stuff with Scout's magic marker . . .

**Scout**   I love stationery.

**Bruce**   Wayne, you can't seriously believe that . . .

**Wayne**   What's it say, Bruce?

**Bruce** (*reluctantly reading*)   'Delamitri's work is wicked, cynical exploitation and manipulation of the lowest basest elements of the human psyche. His Oscar nomination is an insult to the dead and bereaved of America.' It won't work Wayne! These columnists are cynical reactionaries pursuing a transparent anti-liberal agenda!

**Farrah**   Jesus, Bruce, enough of this bullshit please, it isn't the time.

**Wayne**   It will work Bruce because you are going to tell the world that me 'n' Scout are weak-willed, simple-minded creatures who have been – what's it say in the *Tribune* there Bruce, just read it out would you –

**Bruce**    '– seduced by Hollywood's pornographic imagery of sex and death.'

**Wayne**    Images *you* create, man! And for which you have just been honoured with an Oscar. You are going to say that your eyes have been opened and you are *ashamed*.

**Scout**    And so you should be by the sound of it.

**Wayne**    In fact, I got an idea, man! Oh yeah! You're going to return your Oscar.

**Bruce**    My Oscar?!

**Wayne**    That's right, you're going to give it back on live TV. Out of respect for your victims. The people *you* killed *through* me and Scout.

**Bruce**    It won't work, Wayne! It can't. Whatever I say or do won't change the law.

**Wayne**    Bullshit, Bruce, and you know it! The law is whatever people want it to be! It ain't never the same thing twice. It's one thing to a white man, another to a black. One thing to the rich and another to the poor. The law is a piece of fuck'n' Play Dough, no-one knows what shape it's going to be in next. Man, after you've made your broadcast me, and Scout here, won't be no punk killers no more. We'll be hundred things, we'll be heroes to some, victims to others, we'll be monsters, we'll be saints. We will be the defining fuck'n' image of a national debate! A debate that'll go to the core of our society.

**Scout**    Don't you just love it when he talks like that? I don't know where he gets all that stuff.

**Wayne**   TV, honey. A man can pick up a lot of fancy-sounding bullshit if he watches TV all his life.

**Bruce**   Wayne, listen to yourself, defining fucking image, for Christ's sake! Who do you think you are. You're a punk, a dirty little punk.

**Velvet**   Daddy, be nice!

**Wayne**   Come on, man! It doesn't get any better than this. The King of Hollywood, two mass murderers, a dying *Playboy* centrefold, a rinsed out hag of an ex-wife, a spoilt, sexy little weeping teen – blood, guns – we've got it all. Nobody will ever forget this, it will be burned on their minds forever, and every time anyone sees you, Bruce, they'll remember you with your arms round me and Scout, Brooke dying at your feet saying: 'America, wake up! We sow a wind and we reap a whirlwind.'

*The phone rings.*

Honey! Get the phone.

**Scout** (*into the phone*)   Hallo. . . . My name is Scout, how may I help you?

**Wayne** (*grabbing the phone*)   You got the crew?

**Scout** (*to* **Velvet**)   That's how they take calls in motels, I think it's nice. All Wayne ever says is 'yeah'.

**Wayne**   Yeah. I'm coming down, OK, Bruce, you just start thinking about what I told you because I guess you know what I'll do if you don't, that is if'n Scout hasn't done it already. See you in five, baby.

**Scout**   I'll be here waiting for you, hunk.

*They embrace and* **Wayne** *exits.*

*They all sit.* **Scout***'s guns are much in evidence.*

Ain't Wayne smart, huh?

**Bruce**    Not if he thinks I'm going to do this thing for him, he isn't smart at all.

**Scout**    Oh you'll do it. You ain't boss here any more.

**Bruce**    You think I'm going to buy into this circus! This media feeding frenzy! I won't. I can't. There is such a thing as creative integrity, you know.

*With a supreme effort* **Brooke** *speaks up.*

**Brooke**    I have been shot!

**Velvet**    Don't talk Brooke, it puts pressure on your wound.

**Brooke**    He's worrying about his fucking image.

**Bruce**    Hey Brooke, I didn't shoot you and I have stuff to think about here too! I know you're hurt bad and when I can do something to help you I will. Right now however, I am powerless . . .

**Velvet**    You don't have to go on about your creative integrity though, Dad. I mean it's kind of gross.

**Bruce**    I'm thinking about the social implications of this thing. What they are asking is immoral, it's obscene. – They want me to make excuses for murder. – Already people pass the buck for just about everything, from drink driving to –

**Farrah**    Jesus! Back with that. Can't you change the record, Bruce.

**Bruce**    I will not be a party to the further immoralization of America!

**Farrah**    Bruce, you're such an asshole.

**Velvet**    Immoralization is not a word.

**Farrah**   No wonder the Democrats never invite you to
their conventions no matter how much money you give
them.

**Bruce**   This man wants me to confess to mass murder
on television! I can't do it!

**Scout**   Yes, you can, asshole.

**Velvet**   Dad. Listen to yourself. He's shot Brooke. He
said I'd be good TV if he did whatever, nobody cares
that you don't like it. You have to say it that's all.

**Bruce**   And when I do, I'm dead.

**Brooke**   Ha!

**Bruce**   Well, not actually dead, but dead both morally
and as an artist. Listen baby, I won't let him hurt you,
I've got to think this through. That bastard doesn't just
want to destroy what I am, but what I've been!
Everything I've done and achieved. He wants me to say
my whole life has been a piece of pornography.

**Farrah**   So what? Who cares?

**Bruce**   So what? So fucking what! My life work,
Farrah! My legacy, belittled and soured. That scumbag,
that shit!

**Scout**   You'd better watch your mouth.

**Bruce**   What? You want me to like the guy, Scout?
Your boyfriend is a sadistic maniac, a heartless
psychopath.

**Scout**   You don't know his nice side.

**Bruce**   I have a duty as a public figure here!

**Farrah**   Hey Bruce, here's an idea, how about you
shut your dumb mouth for a minute, huh?

**Bruce**   What?

**Farrah**   We're all tired of your bullshit and there are practical considerations here.

**Bruce**   Practical considerations, what, more practical than my life?

**Brooke**   Ha!

**Farrah**   Listen – Miss – Scout? I'd like to ask you a favour – would it be all right if my husband made a call? Or maybe sent a fax.

**Scout**   It depends . . .

**Bruce**   What the hell's on your mind, Farrah?

**Farrah**   Bruce, think about it. So what if this thing ruins you as an artist? Who gives a fuck. It's time you got a life anyway. The real point is it will completely destroy you financially.

**Velvet**   Mom!

**Farrah**   Once you claim responsibility for inciting murder, the families of every victim of violence in America are going to sue the living ass off you. The criminals too come to think of it! What we have to do right now is transfer your assets and property into my name. If Miss Scout here will let you make a call . . .

**Velvet**   Mom! For God's sake!

**Farrah**   Lady I am protecting your future.

**Scout**   You're quite something aren't you?

**Farrah**   I just don't happen to want some Milwaukee waitress whose husband got knifed in a bar getting hold of my money.

**Scout**    Well he ain't gonna make no call. So I guess you'll just have to think about being poor.

**Farrah**    Poor, oh my God.

**Scout**    Personally I reckon maybe that waitress in Milwaukee would have a point. Maybe your damn high and mighty moral husband shouldn't have made the films he did.

**Bruce**    What did you say?

**Scout**    Well you know, films and TV, they used to be an escape from being poor and living in fear, now they just rub your nose in it.

**Bruce**    Well don't go then, you can watch *The Waltons* on cable.

**Velvet**    Daddy don't be so patronizing.

**Scout**    I mean you live in a big old house in Hollywood and you pay for it by making films that show real people, people who live in ghettos and trailer parks, look ugly and sick and violent . . .

**Bruce**    You are ugly and sick and violent!

**Farrah**    Bruce!

**Bruce**    Well . . .

**Scout**    I know I am, I know that, and I deserve whatever I get . . . It just seems to me that half of America is living in hell for the entertainment of the other half.

**Wayne** *enters, accompanied by* **Bill** *and* **Kirsten** *who are a small camera crew, in their underwear. Obviously they are very nervous. They carry a camera, camera stand, boom microphone, ratings monitor, headphones, radios etc.*

**Wayne**  OK everybody we're getting somewhere here. It's media city out there Bruce – The Wayne and Scout Village! We got every damn network 'cept the Home Shopping channel and I guess they may not be long.

**Scout**  I love that shopping channel. The way they can just keep on talking about a little bracelet or a nutmeg grinder.

**Wayne**  Honey, not now.

**Scout**  I mean, sometimes, you didn't even know you wanted a musical vegetable shredder.

**Wayne**  Honey, *not now.* This is Bill and Kirsten, they are going to send our message to the nation – I sincerely apologize for the working conditions – OK Bruce you're the director. Where should these people stick their camera? . . .

**Bruce** *is now angry and confused enough to be reckless.*

**Bruce**  You know where you can stick it, Wayne.

**Velvet**  Daddy for Christ's sake!

**Bruce**  He isn't going to shoot me Velvet, he needs me.

**Velvet**  He doesn't need me!

**Wayne**  That's true enough, young lady, you tell your daddy.

**Bruce**  I've told you you'll get nothing from me if you hurt her.

**Wayne**  Well anyways, I guess I can do this myself. Maybe I'll get an Oscar too ha ha! – OK, I reckon you guys can set up down there – well come on we haven't got all day, chop chop, ha – Chop Chop.

**Bill** *and* **Kirsten** *set up* DSC *with their backs to the audience.*

OK now, I think I got my visual concept together here –
you like that Scout, visual concept'?

**Scout**    You know I love it honey.

**Wayne**    If we see this area here as kind of centre of the
action – Scout move that coffee table.

**Scout**    I ain't touching that coffee table. (*To* **Farrah**
*and* **Velvet**.) You move it.

**Wayne**    I'll just get Brooke here into the picture.

**Wayne** *drags* **Brooke** *to the front of the sofa.* **Brooke** *cries
out in pain.*

Now don't make such a fuss, Brooke – there see, she
looks great lying on the floor there, don't she? Like some
kind of wounded swan or something.

**Velvet**    She's dying.

**Velvet** *puts her jacket or a coat over* **Brooke**.

**Wayne**    We're all dying darlin' from the day we're
born. What I'm saying is that her pathetic condition
kind of underlines the point I'm making here. So get
that coat off her, sugar, it ain't cold and it's spoiling my
picture. Ain't nothing sexy 'bout a coat.

**Velvet** *takes the coat off* **Brooke**.

**Kirsten**    Mr Hudson.

**Wayne**    Yeah?

**Kirsten**    May I place this boom mike here?

**Wayne**    Sure you can ma'am – OK, this thing's really
coming together now. So how about you, what can we
do with you?

**Wayne** *looks at* **Farrah**.

**Farrah**   What do you mean?

**Wayne**   This is TV, honey, good look'n' woman like
you's gonna be a big draw, particularly 'long side of
your cute li'l daughter! – Scout baby, take Mrs
Delamitri and Miss Delamitri and 'cuff them to them
pillars up yonder.

**Scout**   Sure will, Buffalo Bill.

**Wayne**   C'mon, get over there girls, we ain't making
*Gone With the Wind* here, this is live action . . .

**Scout** *gets some handcuffs from* **Wayne**'s *bag.* **Scout**
*manacles* **Farrah** *and* **Velvet** *to the pillars.*

Excuse me partner, would it be OK if I took a look
through the lens?

**Bill**   You're the director, sir.

**Wayne**   Well that's right, I guess I am.

**Wayne** *struts over and looks through the lens.*

OK now, Bruce'll be in the middle, Scout – now you
sure you're going to be able to get all this in, Bill? What
is your 'edge of frame' . . .

**Scout**   'Edge of frame', did you hear that? 'Edge of
frame'. Wayne you are so cool.

**Wayne**   I know baby, I know.

**Bill**   We have plenty of width. I've just locked it off,
we'll take the whole thing in a static six shot, sir. Have
another look, sir.

**Wayne**   I don't know, there just seems to be a certain
someth'n' missing.

**Wayne** *crosses to* **Velvet**. *He studies her for a moment and then rips open* **Velvet**'s *top*.

**Scout**   Wayne, take your hands off that girl right now!

**Wayne**   You want the ratings honey? Huh? You want people to watch this thing? Sex is important on TV, sex sells.

**Wayne** *pulls at* **Velvet**'s *blouse, exposing her shoulders*.

Cute huh? Can't show too much, of course, there's strict rules. Just enough for the couch potatoes out there in TV land to get themselves off on . . .

**Farrah**   Don't be scared honey – you look great.

**Wayne**   OK, I guess we're just about ready – so you get up there, Bruce, and get ready to tell America what I said to tell them.

**Bruce** *has been thinking hard, desperately looking for a way out*.

**Bruce**   Wayne, this isn't going to work. All it will do is screw my life up forever . . .

**Wayne**   Well, that's a shame Bruce, because it's the best shot I've got and we're going to try it . . .

**Farrah**   Just do it, Bruce.

**Velvet**   Yes, Daddy, just do it.

**Brooke**   Yeah, do it.

**Bruce**   I'm doing it, for God's sake! I just think there's a better way here Wayne, better for you as well as me.

**Wayne**   Well, if there is, Bruce, I'd be pleased to hear it but I have to tell you that me 'n' Scout have considered every option.

**Bruce**   I think you should debate me.

**Wayne**  Debate you?

**Bruce**  You're not stupid, Wayne, and neither is
Scout. You know that the best you have here is a long
shot. You know that me claiming responsibility for your
actions while you hold a gun to my daughter's head, is
not really going to cut a lot of ice. So debate me.

**Scout**  You be careful, Wayne.

**Bruce**  Come on, Scout, remember that stuff you were
saying earlier. About me exploiting the ugly and the
downtrodden, how I get rich leeching off the suffering of
the poor.

**Wayne**  D'you say that, baby doll?

**Scout**  Yes, I did, and I meant it and so did the guy I
saw saying it on 'Sixty Minutes'.

**Bruce**  Well that's a better argument than just using
me as some kind of puppet. Put your case. Establish my
guilt and let me deny it.

**Scout**  Don't do it darling, your plan's better; just
make him say the stuff you said.

**Bruce**  Think of your image, Scout. What do you
want that camera to see? A couple of sullen thugs or
good-looking, in your face, anti-heroes. By tomorrow
morning, you'll be on a million T-shirts, you'll be able to
name your price. You'll be stars.

**Scout**  Seems to me we're already stars.

**Kirsten** *has her earphones on.*

**Kirsten**  Uhm – boss, they want to know what's going
on, are we going to give them some pictures or not?

**Bruce**  Come on, Wayne. Or maybe you don't have
the balls.

**Wayne**    Oh, I've got the balls, Bruce. I got all the balls, including yours.

**Wayne** *grabs* **Bruce**'*s balls viciously.* **Bruce** *yelps in agony.*

I don't like being goaded, Bruce. Don't ever think you can goad me – but OK, let's do it. Let's have us a debate.

**Wayne** *releases* **Bruce.** **Kirsten** *speaks into her radio.*

**Kirsten**    Vision control, stand by, we're going to give you pictures.

**Bruce** (*in pain*)    And then will you let Farrah and Velvet go? Will you let Brooke get to a doctor?

**Wayne**    I never know what I'll do, Bruce – it's my job, I'm a maniac.

**Kirsten**    They're ready in vision control . . .

**Scout**    Oh Wayne, I look a sight. Can't they send someone in from make-up?

**Wayne**    You look gorgeous, baby.

**Scout**    I do not.

**Wayne**    Brooke did your hair just peachy. Sit down. OK, are you ready, Bruce?

**Bruce**    I still have some discomfort.

**Wayne**    Well that's showbiz. Ya gotta suffer for it. OK Kirsten.

**Kirsten**    OK, we are going to take this thing in *five*, four, three, two, one. And we are live across America.

**Wayne**    No offence, but I think I'll just check we ain't talking to ourselves . . .

**Wayne** *points the remote at the TV . . . Clearly they can see that* *they are on it. We hear **Wayne**'s next speech with an echo on it because it's also coming out of the TV.*

That's us honey! We're on TV! We're on TV!

**Scout** *screams.*

OK, I'll just mute the sound here . . .

**Wayne** *and* **Scout** *are somewhat transfixed by the TV. They experiment with moving their arms. After a moment **Bruce** clears his throat. **Wayne** remembers the job at hand.*

Right, OK, here we are, uhm, Bruce it's your house, maybe you'd better say hi.

**Bruce**    All right Wayne. I will. (*To the camera.*) Hallo everybody. I am sorry to interrupt your morning viewing but I guess you all know what's going on here. I'm Bruce Delamitri, the Oscar-winning film maker. The two women you see manacled behind me are Farrah, my wife and our daughter Velvet.

**Velvet**    Please, *Dad.*

**Bruce**    The wounded woman on the floor is Brooke Daniels, the mode. . . .

*A croak from **Brooke**.*

I'm sorry, actress. We are all prisoners of Wayne Hudson, whom you see here, and his partner, Scout.

**Wayne**    Howdy y'all.

**Scout**    Hallo America.

**Bruce**    So let us come to the point. I make films in which actors and stunt artists pretend to kill people. Wayne and Scout actually kill people. They are of course the notorious Mall Murderers and they claim that I am responsible for their actions, that my work has somehow inspired them.

**Scout**   We never said you'd inspired us Mr Delamitri, now don't you go putting words into our mouths.

**Wayne**   Yeah, it ain't like we saw a guy and a girl shooting people in your movie and said 'Hell, I never thought of that, that's what we should be doing.'

**Bruce**   So my work doesn't inspire you? (*To the camera.*) You hear that America, it doesn't inspire them! – Well forgive me Wayne but I can't imagine what other point you're making when you equate me with your disgusting and sickening crimes.

**Wayne**   It ain't a direct thing, Bruce! We ain't morons! We didn't walk straight out of 'Ordinary Americans' and shoot the popcorn seller . . .

**Scout**   Actually we did, Wayne.

**Wayne**   Once! That's all, we did that once! I must have seen that movie fifty times, and only once did we walk out and shoot the popcorn seller. Besides which nobody shoots a popcorn seller in 'Ordinary Americans'? Do they Bruce?

**Bruce**   I don't believe so.

**Wayne**   You don't believe damn right. Fifty-seven people get shot in 'Ordinary Americans'.

**Scout**   Wayne counted them.

**Wayne**   Of course I counted them, honey pie, or how would I know ? They don't put it up on the titles do they? Like that damn movie you liked – 'Marrying and Dying' . . .

**Scout**   *Four Weddings and a Funeral*. I loved that movie. It must be so great to be English, everything's so elegant and nice.

**Wayne**   Yeah, well, Bruce here did not call his movie 'Fifty-seven Murders plus People Taking Drugs and Fucking' did he, the point is –

**Scout**   Wayne you can't use the F word on live TV.

**Kirsten**   That's OK, they're using a beeper.

**Bruce**   The point is, Wayne, as you yourself have observed, no popcorn seller gets shot in my movie. There's no damn cause and effect here. You see my stuff but you do your stuff, end of story. You'd have killed that guy if you'd just walked out of *Mary Poppins*!

**Wayne**   I guess I probably would at that.

**Bruce**   Of course you would! You are your own man, aren't you? Are you a man, Wayne?

**Wayne**   Of course I'm a man!

**Bruce**   And you do what you want!

**Wayne**   Yes I do.

**Bruce**   Nobody pushes you around, not cops, not hoods and certainly not any damn movie!

**Wayne**   Bruce, I see what you're getting at but you're twisting this thing all around.

**Bruce**   No, I am not.

**Wayne**   Yes, you are.

**Scout**   I don't like this debate! You make him say what you planned, Wayne! Make him read out that newspaper stuff.

**Wayne**   There ain't nothing specific here, I am talking generally.

**Bruce**   Oh generally! Well that's very convenient isn't it. (*To the camera.*) You hear that! (*Back to* **Wayne**.) Pretty

much covers every eventuality doesn't it? You've
screwed up and you feel somehow or other, generally
speaking, someone else should take the blame. Me!
Society! Who cares, it doesn't matter as long as it isn't
you. Now where did I hear that before? Maybe from
every failure there ever was. Isn't it funny how nobody
ever seems to give society the credit when they succeed!

**Wayne**   Tell me something, Bruce, I've always wanted
to know. Do you get a hard-on when you make your
movies?

**Bruce**   That is such a cheap shot.

**Wayne**   'Cos I admit it, that stuff just thrills me – and
I look round the movie theatre and I can see all the
other guys and they're just loving it. Everyone of them is
just itching to haul out a gun and blast away. Of course
they don't do it but I can see them licking their lips just
the same. It's beautiful, you make killing cool.

**Bruce**   No, Wayne. I make going to the movies cool.

**Wayne**   *Exactly*! I'm talking about a culture that (*He
checks one of the newspapers; reading.*) 'celebrates and exploits
violence'. We're all livin' it, breathin' it, getting off on it
every day and it ain't only the criminals who create it.

**Bruce**   It's only the criminals who commit the crimes!
Violent people create a violent society. They do it, not
me, not anyone else. They are to blame. You are to
blame and you alone!

**Scout**   Now are you sure about that, Mr Big Shot
Director?

**Velvet**   Yes, are you sure, Daddy?

**Farrah**   Velvet keep out of this and don't slouch!

**Scout**   Are you sure? Are you sure that no matter how

many times you show a sexy murder to a rock and roll soundtrack you ain't eventually going to get into peoples' brains?

**Bruce**    I don't know! I don't know the answer to that! I cannot and will not attempt to second guess the unknowable reactions of criminally insane maniacs! Does *Hamlet* encourage regicide? Does *Oedipus* make people sleep with their mothers?

**Scout** (*shocked*)    Well there is no call for that type of talk!

**Bruce** (*to the camera*)    Cars kill people, you going to ban cars! Booze kills people, maybe we should all sue Jack Daniels! Do movies kill? Probably not, but let's ban them anyway. Then we can put all the directors in prison for murder and the murderers can go on Oprah and tell us how Hollywood made them dysfunctional!

**Wayne**    Fifty-seven murders Bruce, you ever hear of a little boy named Pavlov and his dog.

**Kirsen** *looks up from her screen.*

**Kirsten**    Excuse me – uhm, this is all very interesting of course, and the producers are delighted, they're *very* happy in control – but I can see here from my ratings monitor that the main channels are losing viewers. They want to know in control whether it would be OK to record this and edit it for the evening news.

**Wayne**    No! I have an idea.

**Wayne** *shouts into the camera.*

Hey America! Listen, phone your friends, tell them to tune in, because in sixty seconds I'm going to shoot Farrah Delamitri, in sixty seconds she will be one dead mutha!

**Farrah**    No!!

*Everybody screams and protests.*

**Bruce**    Wayne!

**Velvet**    Please, she's my mom!

**Bruce**    How can more killing possibly help your case?

**Wayne**    How are the ratings Kirsten?

**Kirsten**    Yep, they've leapt, but my producer is saying don't kill the woman.

**Wayne**    Is that what he's saying? Well I don't notice him turning off his cameras.

**Kirsten**    He says he has no right to censor the news.

**Wayne**    Well, that's pretty fucking convenient, particularly since we're making the news for his benefit!

**Bruce**    Turn off the broadcast! Turn off the broadcast, turn it off . . .

**Wayne**    Scout, get him out of the way. Hurry up now y'all. You don't want to miss it do ya? – Five four three two one!

**Wayne** *shoots* **Farrah**. *She falls dead, still chained to the pillar.*

**Bruce**    You bastard! When will this end?

**Wayne**    You saw the ratings, man.

**Bruce**    You hypocritical swine! *You* killed her, no-one else! What is it you're saying? That the media, the public is responsible for the fact that you're a murdering lunatic?

**Wayne**    I'm just saying I wouldn't 'a shot her if people hadn't turned over to another channel.

That's all. You work it out.

**Bruce**    You are responsible!

**Wayne**    Yes! I am responsible for me, but you are responsible for you and they are responsible for them. I don't see anyone doing much about that. I've got an excuse, I'm a psycho, what's your get-out?

**Kirsten** *receives a message from the producer. She turns to* **Bill**.

**Kirsten**    Bill, get down!

**Bill**    What?

**Kirsten**    The police are coming in!

**Kirsten** *and* **Bill** *dive down.* **Wayne** *shouts into the camera.*

**Wayne**    No! Wait! Hold it. I'll give myself up, Scout too! I swear! Stop the attack, Bill, Bill, Bill is this camera rolling?

**Bill**    Yes sir.

**Wayne**    We'll give up! But we give ourselves up to the people. The people are responsible. They decide our fate, the fate of everybody in this room.

**Wayne** *has pushed* **Scout** *to grab the ratings monitor. She does so and hands it to him.* **Wayne** *puts it by* **Brooke**'s *head.*

It's up to you, the people out there – the lives of us all are in your hands. Here's how it is. When I've finished talking, if everybody watching switches off their TV, I swear me and Scout will walk out of here with our hands up – But if you keep on watching, I will kill every last mutha in this room, including myself and Scout. Not a bad show huh? Exciting, right? And to see it, all you have to do is stay tuned for another few seconds – well, you're responsible, are you gonna turn off your TV?

*Black-out.*

*When ready bring up general lighting.*

*The cast assemble on stage and take their bows.*

*After a decent curtain call but before the applause has died some sort of change of lighting state occurs. Perhaps a red wash and a spotlight on* **Bruce**. *Something to tell the audience, who had been about to leave, that there is something else. The actors tell their stories, remaining in character.*

**Bruce**   Bruce Delamitri survived Wayne's bloody TV show but his career never recovered. He now makes tired, cynical movies in France. He has written a book about the night Wayne and Scout entered his life, called 'I Am Not Responsible'.

**Brooke**   Brooke died of her wounds. Her parents claim that by pursuing his debate Bruce denied Brooke the medical care that could have saved her. They are suing him.

**Kirsten**   Bill and Kirsten both died in the police assault. Their families are suing the television companies, whom they claim had a duty of care to their employees.

**Bill**   They are also suing the police whom they claim should have intervened earlier.

**Kirsten**   In a separate claim they are suing the police for intervening at all.

**Velvet**   Velvet was also killed in the crossfire. In the largest single claim in history her grandparents are suing the people who did not turn off their TVs.

**Karl**   The people who did not turn off their TVs have experienced stress and mental torment as a result of the terrible moral dilemma that the TV companies allowed them to be put in. They have formed themselves into action groups and are pursuing claims for damages.

**Farrah**    The TV companies claim that in the final analysis only government can be responsible for how public amenities operate. They are looking to Washington to underwrite their losses.

**Wayne**    Wayne Hudson died in the gun battle with the police. His parents are pursuing the Social Services Department claiming that it was their early neglect that was responsible for turning Wayne bad. Scout's parents are also suing the Social Services claiming that their early intervention made Scout what she was.

**Scout**    Scout survived the gun fight and was eventually sent to a secure mental hospital where she has discovered religion. She feels that the Almighty does all things for a purpose and that in the long run God is responsible for everything.

**Bruce**    So far no-one has claimed responsibility.

*Black-out.*